TRADING UNDER SAIL
OFF JAPAN, 1860–99

FRONTISPIECE: A Japanese drawing of
Captain Will, used by him as his bookplate.
The inscription reads:
'The Captain San-shaku ["Shorty"] whom I greatly respect.
(my picture)'

TRADING UNDER SAIL OFF JAPAN, 1860-99

THE RECOLLECTIONS OF

CAPTAIN JOHN BAXTER WILL

SAILING-MASTER & PILOT

EDITED

WITH A HISTORICAL INTRODUCTION

By GEORGE ALEXANDER LENSEN

SOPHIA UNIVERSITY · TOKYO

IN COOPERATION WITH

THE DIPLOMATIC PRESS

TALLAHASSEE, FLORIDA

PUBLISHED BY

SOPHIA UNIVERSITY

7, KIOI-CHŌ, CHIYODA-KU

TOKYO

IN COOPERATION WITH

THE DIPLOMATIC PRESS, INCORPORATED

2305 AMELIA CIRCLE, TALLAHASSEE, FLORIDA

Library of Congress Catalog Card No. 68-26390

PRINTED AND BOUND IN JAPAN

PETER BROGREN, THE VOYAGERS' PRESS, TOKYO

TO THE EDITOR'S FRIENDS

IN HAKODATE

WHO MAKE EVERY VISIT

A HOMECOMING

CONTENTS

LIST OF ILLUSTRATIONS

INTRODUCTION

FROM the seventeenth century to the mid-nineteenth, Japan sought peace in isolation. American and Russian gunboats pierced her seclusion and prodded her back into the maelstrom of international relations. By the summer of 1859 four Japanese ports were open to Western commerce: Hakodate, Shimoda, Nagasaki and Kanagawa (Yokohama). But the opening of Hyōgo (Kobe) and Niigata or another suitable harbor on the west coast, set by treaty for 1863 and 1860 respectively, and the admission of Western residents to the capital city of Edo (now Tokyo) and to Osaka, slated for 1862 and 1863, had to be postponed for half a decade because of internal opposition to Western inroads. The rest of the country remained *terra incognita* to most foreigners until 1894, when a series of new treaties between Japan and the powers guaranteed reciprocal rights of travel and residence.

The opening of the country had become a political issue within Japan. It was used by the Imperialists as a club to knock down the military dictatorship of the Tokugawa Shogunate which had signed the early treaties. Though the Imperial goverment, upon the Restoration of imperial authority, adopted the very policy the Shogunate had pursued, the anti-foreignism which it had fanned to embarrass its political opponents could not so readily be stilled. Now and again Western visitors (and pro-Western Japanese) were cut down by die-hard samurai.

The momentous changes which Japan experienced in the second half of the nineteenth century made this one of the most fascinating periods in her history. It also made it one of her most important, for in it was shaped the Japan that was to burst forth so forcefully in the twentieth century. Eyewitness recollections of Westerners who observed the changes and contributed to them are, therefore, of considerable interest.

TRADING UNDER SAIL OFF JAPAN

In the Municipal Library of Hakodate, one of the first Japanese ports to be opened, there are a number of unpublished manuscripts relating to the northern regions of Japan. Among them there are two large notebooks (one written in pen, one in pencil), collectively entitled "Looking Back." They are the memoirs of John Baxter Will, a Scotch navigator, captain, trader and later constable and perhaps vice consul of the British legation in Hakodate, who worked in and out of Hakodate for most of his life. The memoirs cover the period from 1860 to 1899, practically from the opening of Japan to Western commerce to the end of the nineteenth century.

Captain Will was a pioneer in the development of Western navigation and commerce in northern Japan. No one knew the waters between Japan and China better than he; no one could handle a sailing vessel in these parts of the world with greater assurance than he. He held both English and Japanese master certificates. He worked with Japanese seamen and taught them how to run Western ships until they were good enough to replace him.

'Old Will,' as he often called himself, was an 'old salt,' not a man of letters. His memoirs are best read aloud, for Will, like many a mariner, was a colorful talker. His memoirs are not only entertaining, however; they are a social document, significant for the light they throw on the daily activities of the Western mariners and merchants along the coasts of Japan and China in the second half of the nineteenth century and on their dealings with the local inhabitants. Will was eyewitness, furthermore, to such historic events as the naval battle of Hakodate, which effectively ended the civil war in 1869. His description of the colonization of Sakhalin and of the seasonal labor on Itorup (Etorofu) offer fresh perspectives on this field.

We know little about Captain Will, except what he tells us himself in his notebooks. He was born in 1840, thus was about twenty years old when he first visited Japan. He was a Scot and proud of it. He had a strong constitution and even stronger personality. He had no hesitation about telling his superiors how to run a ship and did not shrink from taking the pay of a captain for whom he substituted,

Introduction

qualities which in the end gained him more enemies than admirers. His memoirs close in 1899 with his appointment as constable of the British legation in Hakodate. He makes no mention of getting married, but the manuscript was presented to the Municipal Library of Hakodate by Mr. Sakai Chōjirō, who is said to have been his Japanese nephew (son of the sister of Mrs. Will). It is likely that Will took a wife after he settled down as constable, i.e. upon completion of his memoirs.

Mr. Sakai deposited in the Municipal Library of Hakodate also a handwritten copy and a Japanese translation of the original manuscript. From him, I suppose, the library also obtained the information that Will eventually became vice consul of Great Britain, though there is no record of this in the Foreign Office Archives in Tokyo.

The manuscript was written in about 1900; it was given to the Municipal Library of Hakodate some twenty-one years later. I first came across it during my research in Hakodate in 1953-54. I ran into it again in December of 1967 and this time could not resist the temptation to edit it. Not only does it supplement the observations of fin-de-siècle Japan that I have already published, but it fits naturally into the stream of books appearing in Japan in commemoration of the centennial of the Meiji Restoration.

As editor I have taken a number of liberties with the manuscript. The original, except for the division into two notebooks, formed one enormous unit with no paragraphs and only infrequent and inadequate punctuation. I have broken the text up into chapters, paragraphs and sentences. I have also changed the title from 'Looking Back' to something more descriptive. I have corrected spelling errors as a matter of course. For example, Will usually confused 'there' and 'their'. To have supplied proper spellings in brackets or to have put 'sic' after every error would have made the book unreadable. I have tried to preserve the flavor of the original by not correcting grammatical errors or completing sentences unless required for the sake of clarity. I have decapitalized most words and have deleted some of Will's countless 'and' and 'so,' replacing them with semicolons. Needless to say, the purpose of all my editorial changes has been to clarify Will's observations, never to modify them.

The sort of changes that were made in the manuscript for the sake of clarity are best illustrated by an example. Will was explaining how he managed to lift the boiler of a railway engine from shore aboard ship without proper equipment and how the captain was unable to bring his ship to anchor properly—two unrelated ideas that somehow got jumbled together. The manuscript stated:

> Seeing that a watch tackle could do all that was needed we lashed the topsail yard to the lower mast head the Halyards which were on that Side the ship put a strop round the Boiler hooked the Halyards on and with 2 Men pulling the Boiler was level now the trouble came there were only 2 Steam winches and their Power was not equal to the lift so we had to lead the Main lifting gear to the Steam Windlass so after faring up on the Donkey Boiler all it would Stand we got the Boiler and some trucks on board started for Tsuruga here again we had trouble he was one of them men who always wanted his anchor buoyed proper thing to do only his Idea of bringing his ship to anchor at Tsuruga we had the whole harbour some Square Miles of it to ourselves, he would go astern stop the ship dead with a turn ahead this brought the bouy rope in a coil right under the anchor Several times he had done this before let go the anchor of course it fouled the bouy rope anchor gone the bouy was not Visible then the anchor had to be hove up and bouy cleared then ahead and astern and the bouy rope coil under the anchor again let go I called out to him that the bouy was still foul of the anchor give a turn of the Engine either way to clear the rope no let go the anchor.

The passage was changed to read:

> Seeing that a watch tackle could do all that was needed, we lashed the topsail yard to the lower mast head and the halyards which were on that side of the ship. We put a strop round the

boiler, hooked the halyards on, and with two men pulling, the boiler was level. Now the trouble came. There were only two steam winches and their power was not equal to the lift, so we had to lead the main lifting gear to the steam windlass. After firing up on the donkey boiler all it would stand, we got the boiler and some trucks on board. Started for Tsuruga.

Here again we had trouble.

He was one of those men who always wanted his anchor buoyed. Proper thing to do except for his idea of bringing his ship to anchor. At Tsuruga we had the whole harbour—some square miles of it—to ourselves. He would go astern, stop the ship dead with a turn ahead; this brought the bouy rope in a coil right under the anchor. The several times he had done this before [he] let go the anchor. Of course, it fouled the bouy; anchor gone, the bouy was not visible. Then the anchor had to be hove up and the bouy cleared, then ahead and astern, and the bouy rope coil under the anchor again let go. I called out to him that the bouy was still foul of the anchor.

'Give a turn of the engine either way to clear the rope, do not let go the anchor.'

I am grateful to my old friends Miss Okada Hiroko and Mr. Tabata Kōzaburō for bringing the manuscript to my attention and to Mr. Fukuda Isao, director of the Municipal Library of Hakodate, for permission to edit it for publication. Mr. Tabata also photographed most of the illustrations in this book from originals in the collection of the Municipal Library of Hakodate.

The picture of Enomoto Buyō watching the naval battle of Hakodate is from the collection of the Historiographical Institute of the University of Tokyo. It was made available through the courtesy of Professor Numata Jirō. Mr. Carl H. Boehringer, Executive Director of the American Chamber of Commerce in Japan, graciously let me use his woodblock prints of the warship *Kanyei* in Hakodate harbor and of a Russian and an American in Japan at this time.

TRADING UNDER SAIL OFF JAPAN

Mr. Peter Brogren, with whom I discussed practically every sentence in the manuscipt, was of invaluable help in explaining sailing craft terminology and in analyzing some of Will's unpunctuated phrases to determine where they should be broken. I appreciate the financial assistance of the Florida State University Research Council in obtaining a Xerox copy of the manuscript. Although this book is merely a byproduct of the research for which I received a Senior Fellowship, I must express my indebtedness to the National Endowment for the Humanities for making my return to Japan possible. I am thankful to Mr. Baba Akira of the Kokumin Gaikō Kaikan for assisting me in my search for data about Will's service as vice consul and to Mr. Donald H. Albright of the American Cultural Center in Tokyo for the use of his typewriter.

GEORGE ALEXANDER LENSEN

TOKYO, FEBRUARY 1968

Your Old Friend. J. B. Will.
born on January 12th. 1840.

Plate 1: An autographed portrait of Captain John Baxter Will, probably taken at about the time this account was written. (*Courtesy of the Municipal Library of Hakodate.*)

one

APPRENTICESHIP
OFF THE SCOTTISH COAST

I WAS BORN in the town, now city, of Dundee [Scotland] in the first half of January 1840. Got my schooling at Maxwellton Kirk School; Mr. A. Robertson was the master.

In my 11th year left school and went to work in a manufacturer's warehouse, where I learned warping and lapping. In my 13th year I got restless; would not stay at work, always down at the docks and on board ships. At last my father, seeing I would not settle on shore, agreed to let me go to sea.

In the later part of November 1853 I was bound apprentice for four years to Mr. John Morrison, owner of brig *Marys* of 150 tons register, belonging to Dundee. For the 4 years' service I was to receive as wages £24, divided £4, £4, £6 and £10 for the last year; my father going security for me to the amount of £12 that I would complete my indentures.

The *Marys* was lying at Liverpool, having arrived there from Kronstadt, Russia, being among the last vessels to leave that port before the Russian [Crimean] war was declared. In the middle of December my sea outfit completed, I left Dundee along with the owner by night mail for Liverpool to join the *Marys* at that port.

She had almost completed loading a general cargo for Genoa, mostly railway material and, as this was in preplimsol days, there was not much of the vessel's side out of the water.

A

THE accommodation for the crew of six people was a house
built on the after deck, some 10 feet long and 8 feet wide.
Inside this space the crew with their belongings had to eat,
sleep, dress as well as keep their weeks' store of provisions.
Three common sailor chests in the house left barely room for
six pairs of feet on the deck so the boys as a rule had to stand
out and serve the A.B.'s [able-bodied seamen].

Our crew consisted of captain, mate, 2 apprentices and 4
seamen, one of whom shipped as cook, steward and seaman.
Of course, he could not stop on deck night and day, so I as
youngest apprentice, for 2 years had to do the cooking in my
watch on deck. As far as I can recollect, it did not amount to
much.

The whole cooking utensils consisted of a cast-iron kettle
with spout—this boiled the water for cabin use for coffee or
tea—and for the crew a cast-iron boiler, steam tight, with a
valve on top (I have never seen anything like it). Since in
this was boiled the crew's coffee and tea, it was supposed to be
washed out clean after making the coffee in the morning, but
the cook or his assistant were never very particular about the
washing out at sea. In fact, in bad weather sometimes we had
coffee grounds and tea leaves in the boiler at the same time.
Since there was no spout the lid was taken off and each sailor
dipped in his pannikin, bringing up both coffee grounds and
tea leaves if near the bottom. However, that did not matter;
it took at lot to kill sailors in my younger days.

Besides the above there was a big and small iron boiler;
this was part of the range. In said boilers was cooked the beef
or pork; and in one the pea soup or the duff was boiled on
alternate days; plum duff for the cabin, plain suet duff for the

crew. An oven pan mainly used for roasting coffee beans, a pair of small saucepans for boiling rice or other extras: seven utensils in all, so that the cooking did not need much attention from the number of vessels in use.

Unless when making soup, all the water used was salt water, i.e. boiling salt beef or pork as well as the duff, nothing but salt water. In them days fresh water was all carried in wooden casks, lashed on deck, and had to be looked after carefully.

Looking back to those days I can't help thinking how trust-worthy seamen were. The fresh water was served out daily and though the water was within the reach of any one, the trust was never abused. Kept in casks on deck, and when the water ran short and had to be allowed out, the mate, when he had served the allowance, simply took away the dipper. To make a canvass dipper was a very simple thing and the crew could have helped themselves when the officers were below, yet I must say I never knew the men to do such a thing. Sailors have degenerated since those days.

WE left Liverpool before Christmas and had the usual winter weather in Georges Channel and Bay of Biscay. I was sea sick for 2 days, but they soon cured me of that. If I hid away, they pulled me out and threw me down among the water in the lee scuppers, so I had to get up and move about. Soon got rid of the sickness; rather drastic but effectual cure.

We got to Genoa early spring. After discharging our cargo we sailed in ballast for Palermo. There we filled up both ends of the ship with rags, then went to Girgento and filled up with sulphur for Philadelphia.

I must say here, there was no chronometer in the ship, yet we found our way across the Atlantic right enough, arriving at our port about 1st of July.

As we were in port on the ever glorious 4th of July, our crew all ran or were decoyed away, leaving the wages due behind them.

After discharging our cargo, we were towed some 20 miles farther up the river to a place at that time called Windsor. There we loaded a cargo of anthracite coal for St. Johns, New Brunswick.

As we could not get a crew to ship for the voyage home, we shipped 4 men for the run to St. Johns. Arriving there, they left the ship as soon as the sails were fast.

Cargo of coal out, we loaded a cargo of deals for Queenstown for orders. Shipped four men for the run home again at Queenstown.

We got orders to go to Cork with our cargo and discharge it there. Cargo discharged, we shipped an Irish crew. This was the quietest and most sober crew we had in the *Marys*. From Cork we went to Cardiff. Quite a small port in 1854.

Our captain left us at Cardiff, going home to build a new and larger vessel, and we got a Bideford man as captain.

For the voyage we loaded a cargo of coal for Beirut. All went well on the passage out. From Beirut we went to the island of Cyprus and loaded a cargo of maize (Indian corn) for Queenstown for orders.

OUR new captain turned out to be rather fond of liquor. He not only drank all the captain's allowance but also what was put on board for the crew. After leaving the island of Cyprus, we had unfavourable winds and were nearly four weeks before getting to the Rock of Gibraltar. Previous to getting there, we were short of provisions and boarded 2 ships to beg for food.

At Gibraltar the captain went on shore at once to send provisions, we thought. But he forgot all about the provisions and when the mate went to look for him he could not be found.

On the 3rd day they brought on board a cask of salt beef and one of pork, 2 bags of weevily biscuits—condemned military stores. A few days later an east wind came away, and all the other vessels at anchor in the bay got underweigh and left, but our captain did not turn up. He couldn't be found, so we lost that chance, and it was some ten days later before we got another chance.

The captain came on board, bringing 2 cases of Square Gin with him but no more food. With many a black look aft, we hove up the anchor and set sail. Got through the strait, but bad luck still followed us, and after being out some six weeks and almost in the channel our provisions were all finished. The crew went aft to call the captain to order and ask what he was going to do.

As there was no appearance of a change of wind, it was decided to run back to Lisbon, and the helm was put up for that port. By this time there was literally nothing to eat in the ship, only the cargo of maize. We got to Lisbon and this time two of the crew went on shore and quickly brought fresh provisions. Next day two months' stock of provisions came on board.

Then we left Lisbon, and after some three weeks more got to Queenstown, and got orders again to go to Cork with our cargo. When the crew were paid off at Cork, the captain had to pay every man for the time he was short of provisions. Besides got a reprimand from the marine superintendent.

THE owner came to Cork bringing a new captain with him. He was a brother of the first Captain Anderson, and glad I was to get a change.

We loaded a part cargo of flax in Cork, and left that port for Dundee, where we got some necessary repairs, then left for Boness in the Firth of Forth, where we loaded a cargo of pig iron for Swinemunde in Prussia. Discharged at that town, then went to Memel and loaded a cargo of flax for Dundee. All the Russian ports were closed owing to the war.

Arrived home again. After discharging the cargo, we left for Newcastle; there loaded a cargo of coal for Marseilles. Arrived at Marseilles.

We found the harbor full of American clipper ships, chartered as transports by the French. I have never seen since such a lot of fine looking ships under the American Flag.

Our cargo out, we loaded a general cargo, wines, etc. for Liverpool. On our reaching Molyhead, the Liverpool pilot boarded us and told us the war was finished, that peace had been proclaimed.

ARRIVED at Liverpool, the great salt port, and the Russian ports having been closed for two and a half years we were on the spot in time. They hurried our cargo out and put a cargo of salt on board and hurried us off for Riga.

We had rather a long passage round the north of Scotland, and it must have been the beginning of June when we got to Riga. A lot of vessels from the east coasts had got there before us, but we were the first ship with salt.

On the passage from Liverpool I caught a rather severe touch of fever and ague. Every other day I was laid up and did not enjoy Riga very much. Besides I fell overboard there, and was carried by the stream under the ship's bottom, but was picked up astern of the ship.

While lying at Riga we were moored head on to the floating bridge that crosses the river at that town. One day we were ordered to stop working cargo and to decorate ship as the czar of Russia and the king of Prussia were to cross the bridge as well as some thousands of soldiers of all arms which had been or were to be reviewed by the above two rulers: soldiers home from the Crimea. It took the soldiers some three hours to cross. Then came the czar and king with their staffs. They were in a carriage of four horses, sitting side by side. It was a grand display of men, horses and guns; but everything has an end.

After our salt was discharged, we were taken above the bridge, tied up to the bank, and there we loaded a cargo of flax for Dundee.

[When we] arrived there, the ship's time was up and she had to be reclassed. So she was hauled up on the slip, then slid to one side, and the repairers went to work.

I got a month's leave to get cured of the fever and ague, which still hung on to me. The doctor, a friend of my father's, sent me out to his father's farm, some 10 miles from Dundee. Asked his mother to look after me and feed me on milk principally. I can only say the doctor's instructions were faithfully carried out, for in less than a month I was as well as ever I was, and though I have been in many places since where ague was prevalent, it has never touched me again since.

AFTER being repaired, we left for Burntisland. There loaded a cargo of gas coal for Copenhagen. As it was getting late in the year, we hurried up all we could since after leaving Copenhagen we had to go to Riga and were afraid of the river being frozen before we got there.

As it turned out, when we got to the mouth of the river, the pilot told us we could not get to Riga, but we got two miles inside the bar. Place called the Boldero. Found several other vessels lying there, tied up to the bank. We moored ahead of them.

That night came a severe frost. Next morning we were frozen in solid. Our cargo of linseed came down the river to us over the ice.

When all the vessels had finished loading, they started to cut us out of the ice, as well as the vessels that were at Riga town, so that the whole fleet of vessels got out of the river together.

Our cargo being for Newry in Ireland, we made our way to that port via the north of Scotland. We arrived off the Pentland Firth the evening of the 1st of January 1857. Had rather a long passage among the islands, anchoring mostly at night unless the wind was so fair as to lead through the narrow sounds. Arrived at Newry in January.

Our cargo out, took in ballast and left for Glasgow to load

a general cargo for Genoa. The best part of the Cargo was railway chairs and fish plates, filling up with chemicals. We had a long passage to Genoa. Our cargo out, we loaded a cargo of walnut wood in planks, and a large part was blocked-out musket stocks for the British government. This cargo was for London where we arrived in October.

WHILE at Genoa we three apprentices got into trouble. The two younger lads had trouble on the passage out with the mate in whose watch they were. The mate had been trying to lick the youngest one and the two set on him. Hearing the noise, I went out and found they were softening the mate's head by pounding it on the after-hatch. I did not interfere.

So while in Genoa the bumboats came alongside selling fruit, grapes, and peaches; as we had no money and could get none, we treaked [traded] old shakings (old condemned rope and canvas) for fruit. The mate, hearing of this and having the grudge against us for the licking he got on the passage out, reported it to the captain.

As we three stood together, they didn't dare to lick us and the matter was reported to the British consul, a retired naval officer. He told the captain to bring us on shore before him.

The consul tried to browbeat us, and said to us, when we were called before him, that he had made up his mind to send us to prison. Before a word had been said on either side, as oldest apprentice I asked him if that was not what was commonly called coupar justice [*sic*, perhaps 'cooper' implying barrel head, as in 'drumhead']. Not understanding what coupar justice meant, the mate explained it to him. The consul lost his temper; threw a hand bell at me. I ducked, the bell going over my head, broke the office window.

The outcome of it all was I was sent to jail for 10 days, the youngest lad for 5 days; the other the captain and mate begged off, and he was sent on board with a reprimand.

Now as it happened, the consular chaplain at that time in Genoa was a first cousin of the youngest lad and was also a native of Carnoustie, the village the captain and mate came from. When he heard what had taken place and the cause of it, he went on board and, I heard afterwards, gave both captain and mate an unclerical piece of his mind; wrote the whole story home to the owners. He saw the consul; and told him both sides of the story, which, as I have said, he refused to hear from us—which calmed that gentleman's ire so much that he said if we would apologize to him, he would let us out of jail.

But we had had a good time in jail, nothing to do, plenty of company, and much better food than we got on board ship, and both of us were suffering from sore hands (our finger ends were worn to the bone from lifting cast-iron railway chairs that we had to pick up and lift as far as our arms would reach above our heads).

Looking back, that 10 days in an Italian jail, outside the disgrace, was preferable to the hard work and harder fare on a loaded ship.

On our arrival in London the owner and my father, as well as the captain's wife, were there to meet us, and I don't think after the whole story was told, the captain came off best. The mate was discharged and my indenture which had some six weeks to run was cancelled, signed by the owner as full time.

I WENT HOME by steamer to Dundee. After two weeks at home, I shipped as O.S. [ordinary seaman] in the Brig *Riga*.

Bound to Riga, we left the docks; river pilot on board; the wind strong and fair from the westward. After getting out of the river, the pilot discharged.

All plain sail was set, but with the main course stunsail-gear rove [studsail booms extended beyond the yard arms, i.e., slid out and rigged] on both sides—stunsails bent-on but not set.

There was some trouble about setting the stunsails; being at the wheel I could hear the row, but could not make out what it was about. Anyhow the mate came aft and went below to call the captain to relieve him, I thought, but the captain did not come on deck and I could hear nothing from the men forward.

The wind was freshening, was right aft, and there was plenty of wind, rather much for the sail we were carrying. I don't know how long I stood at the wheel.

The ship was rushing through the water for all she was worth. I was getting tired. It felt as if I had been four hours all by myself on deck. My shouting and thumping on deck with my feet brought no response, and I was afraid to leave the wheel for fear the ship would broach too and get caught aback.

At last I got desperate. After steadying her, I made a run for the house where the men were found, all hands turned in and asleep. Got hold of the first man from the door. It turned out it was the apprentice. Hauled him out of his bunk, ran aft to the wheel again as I heard the sails shaking; got her on her course again. The apprentice came aft to see what was the matter, his head through a hole in his blanket and seemed half raised.

It seems the men had come on board not only with more or less whiskey inside but had brought some in bottles with them.

So much for the men, but what about the captain and mate? The captain I had not seen since the pilot left.

As I had just joined the ship that day, I got the prentice to go below and see what had come to the captain and mate as I had seen neither. He came back and said he had roused the mate, who shortly after came on deck. By this time it was near midnight. I told him I had been at the wheel since 8 o'clock.

He put the prentice to the wheel and we both went to the house to turn out the crew, but before we could manage that, we heard the sails shaking and the wheel spinning round. Running aft we found the prentice lying on deck; he had been hove from the wheel.

However, the rumpus of the sails shaking did more to sober them than anything else, for in five minutes all hands were on deck, including the captain.

Being thus sobered up, they got the sails trimmed, the ship on her course again. As the wind was increasing, sail was shortened, and I got a chance to go below.

After daylight, wind still fresh and fair, we got the ship in order; stunsail gear which had been rove but the sails not set was unrove, and booms rigged in.

ON the 3rd night we had got so far up the Kattegat as the Swin light on the Swedish coast, and two lights showed on the Danish side. On my being relieved from the wheel at 10 o'clock, the mate told me to go down in the hold and get the normans for the windlass, as we expected to get to Elsinore shortly after midnight.

The captain had been called before I left the wheel and was on deck. I believe the course was altered on my relief taking the wheel. Anyhow, I had just got below and got the normans in my hand, when the ship struck heavily on a rock, tearing a large hole in her bottom, the water spurting and striking the deck. I threw the normans down and made for the ladder and got on deck. All hands had jumped on deck.

The rocks we had run on were called the Swin Bottoms.

Then the fun commenced getting the boats out and lighting a flare to let the people on shore know and come to our assistance. Eventually it dawned on them that the ship was hard on the rocks and would not sink and as the sea was smooth there was no present danger. A boat came off from the shore and stood by us.

Word was sent to the acting British consul at Halsingborg [?], the Swedish town opposite Elsinore, who came on board.

After consultation with the captain and people from the shore, the ship was to be left and we were told to pack up our belongings and get into the shore boats to be taken on shore. We were landed at a village under the bluff, on which the lighthouse stood, where we stayed for two days.

Surveyors having come from Elsinore and condemned the vessel the morning after this, six carts were engaged and two men with their belongings were put in each cart and taken to Halsingborg where we stayed one night, and next day crossed by steamer to Elsinore. There we were under the British consul and had to toe the line.

Some few days afterwards a steamer from Kronstadt came along and we were sent on board of her to be taken to West Hartlepool, where she was bound. On arrival at West Hartlepool, we were put on board a train for Newcastle by the agent of the Shipwrecked Mariners & Fishermen's Society. On arrival at Newcastle the agent there met us, took us to a restaurant, where we had our dinner, then back to the station; put [us] on board a train for Edinburgh. Though we arrived late at night, we had to walk to the Sailors' home at Lieth to eat and sleep. After breakfast next morning we crossed the ferry to Burntisland, boarded a train which carried us to Tayport, crossed the ferry train to Dundee, where we arrived all well but very hungry.

THE winter of 1857–58 was a very dull one for sailors. If I recollect right, there was a strike among sailors for higher wages. Anyhow my father was not in a hurry to let me go to sea again after my last experience. So I helped in his work till late spring, when I got restless again and would go to sea.

In early May I shipped in a brig belonging to Arbroath and made a voyage to Kronstadt and back to Dundee. Then I shipped in a bark belonging to Montrose, went to Alloa, loaded a cargo of coal for Kronstadt, again taking a cargo of hemp from there to London.

The captain would have liked the crew he had to go with him on his next voyage to Australia, but all refused, saying there was too much hard work in the ship. So 4 of us shipped in a clipper schooner, called the *Fair City of Perth*, and belonging to that port, on a voyage to Gotenburg and back to London. I shipped as cook, steward and seaman and gave great satisfaction to the captain in that capacity.

When we got back to London, he wanted me to stay on with

him, but as the others were leaving and going by the run home in a Dundee bark, I left and went with them, arriving there about Christmas.

So I saw the New Year at home, and about the middle of February shipped on the bark *Rectitude*, belonging to Wm. Kirkland & Sons, timber merchants, for a voyage to St. Johns, N.B.

We had a long, cold passage out, at one time getting as far as 60° North. In this ship I had the best times I had experienced up till then. She was well manned and the weather was so we could do no work other than was necessary, making and taking in sail and pumping out the ship once a watch. A large warm forecastle to live in, and plenty good Scotch, fresh beef and potatoes on board.

Besides there were so many men on board that I never had a turn at the wheel at night and as a dummy rigged up on the forecastle head kept all the lookouts, times were easy.

The reason she carried so many men were that in loading her cargo of square timber at St. Johns, six winches had to be used and three men to each winch. Labour at that time at St. Johns was very expensive, even when it could be got. We got loaded; on deck we had spare spars, for we were too early in the season to take a proper deck load.

After we got to sea we found out another reason why she carried so big a crew. She leaked so badly that she had to be pumped out every hour, and in heavy weather there was always part of the crew at the pump. However we got home all right.

THE mate, Mr. Kennedy, got command of a bark called the

Stork. She was in London, and he asked me to go with him as 2nd mate. When I went to London to join, found the old 2nd mate was still by her. As he was a married man with a family, I shipped as an A.B. and went the voyage to Riga and back to Dundee.

When Mr. Kennedy had left the *Rectitude*, the 2nd mate, Mr. Anderson, had been promoted to mate, and she was lying in Dundee when we arrived there. Mr. Anderson asked me to go back with him. She was going on a voyage to Dramen in Norway to load a cargo of deal or battens for Dundee again. So I shipped on the *Rectitude*.

We got to a fjord, whose name I forget. We lay at anchor a couple of days. No sign of wind changing, the captain went on shore to telegraph for a tow boat to take us to Dramen.

The boat's crew consisted besides the captain, of the 2nd mate, the carpenter who was the captain's brother, an A.B. who was a nephew of the captain, and a prentice whose time was almost served.

When the boat was hauled up, I went in her. Just before leaving, the mate called me up [out of the boat] and sent the captain in my place. As it turned out this was a lucky change for me.

As they had to run to leeward, the sail was set. A fresh breeze blowing, though having some six miles to go, they got to the place very quick.

The business they went on transacted, they left for the ship again; by this time the wind had increased, with nasty chopping sea, and they could not make way with the oars.

The sail was set and they started to tack to windward, and the boat took a lot of water, in stays [i.e., over the gunwale] the last time. Being nearly half full of water, when the sail filled before way was got on the boat, she lay over, filled, and capsized, throwing all the crew in the water; and as they were all heavily clad, there was not much chance for any of them.

The carpenter, who was a good swimmer, struck out for an island close by. A Norwegian vessel, lying at anchor in sight of the accident, put out a boat and went down to the capsized boat. But when they got there the only remaining part of the crew was 2nd mate and prentice. The latter was held up by some of the gear belonging to the sail, 2nd mate holding on the reel. The other three were gone—the captain, his brother, and his nephew.

They took the two survivors on board their vessel, gave them dry clothing and did what they could for them; sent word of the accident to our ship. As the only boat for rowing was gone, we borrowed the skiff that brought the news. And the mate, with a crew from the ship taking clothes for the rescued men, put off to bring them on board.

On reaching the vessel they were on board, we found the prentice off his head, the 2nd mate pretty well played out. However, we got them in the boat and got back a little late after a hard struggle, the wind having taken off a little.

I may mention here that on that same day a very heavy gale of wind was experienced in England. Many wrecks and loss of life; the most noted was the loss of the Black Ball Liner *Red Jacket* on the Welsh coast with the loss of great many lives.

The mate took charge of the *Rectitude*. A tow boat coming next day, we got to Dramen, and loaded a cargo of battens for Dundee, arriving there early November, 1859. This the last of my short voyages.

B

ON the 22nd of November, I shipped on board the bark *Eva* of Dundee, Captain Mills, for a voyage to Rio de Janeiro; cargo: coal and general. From Rio we were to go round the Horn to the Chincha Islands for a cargo of guano. We got away the following day. We found head winds, and after beating about for some days, and getting as far south as the Farne Islands, head winds still holding, the helm was put up and the ship kept away for the Pentland Firth to go round north of Scotland.

Reaching the firth, we found a fresh westerly gale blowing. Stood across the firth, ran through Longhope, and anchored at Strourness, where we lay for some days. Wind hauling a little, we got out through the Hoy Channel by next day.

We had got as far as the Stacks of Cape Wrath, when it came on to blow a heavy gale from the westward again, and as we were losing ground, the helm was put up again, and we ran for the Pentland Firth again. Here meeting the westerly tide against a westerly gale, our decks were full of water; men almost off their feet. We got through all right.

Running down the east coast, the weather moderated, but afterwards it came on the snow for a day or two. We saw nothing, but on a Sunday afternoon we picked up ourselves on shore on a sandbank.

On the snow stopping and clearing up, we found we were ashore on the Shipwash or Orfordness. The ship had slid on the bank so quietly that the watch below hardly felt her go on, but she was on shore fast enough.

THE next thing to do was to get her afloat again. The boats

were put out; the bank was sounded to see which was the best way to get her off. When that was fixed, the stream anchor and hawser were laid out and hove taut. The next thing was the tides. Night came on; the watch set, the other watch went below. Luckily there was no wind and the sea smooth. Although it had cleared up and we could see the land and lights on shore, no one came near us that night from the shore.

Next morning a lugger came, offering assistance, which was not accepted. I forget, now, all we did, but we got her afloat again without assistance, made sail, and put out between the banks to sea.

I forgot to mention that when we shipped, there were one or two clauses in the articles new to me. One was no swearing allowed, another no washing clothes on Sunday, drinking strictly prohibited on board, etc. However, it came on a dirty night, thick with rain, and as we still were among the banks, did not know when we would get on shore again. As we were not sure of the ship's position, sail was shortened, and it was the idea to keep the ship as near as possible stationary.

When I went to the wheel at 8 p.m., I was told to keep the sails lifting all the time. I had not been long at the wheel when the men began to come aft one or two at a time, go down to the cabin, come up smacking their lips as if they had been getting something good. (I may say here, the 2nd mate was the only officer on deck.)

By and by a man came and relieved me, and I was told to go down to the cabin, where I found the captain and mate making port wine negus on the cabin fire and serving it out. I got a hot drink and went back to the wheel and thought about the clause in the articles, drinking strictly prohibited. Of course, one hot drink of port wine was not likely to hurt a sailor, but looking at the captain and mate, I fancied they had taken several hot drinks. Anyhow during that night I don't recollect seeing either of them on deck on duty. The 2nd mate was the only officer.

It was somehow impressed on the crew that the ship was in a pretty tight place. I know that the tackles were got up and got all ready to put the longboat out and our clothes all more or less packed ready. However, daylight came, the weather cleared a little.

We found the few sails that had been set and kept shaking all night were all to pieces and otherwise she looked like a wreck aloft.

The captain and mate coming on deck and seeing the state the ship was in, held a consultation and decided to run to Lowestoft for repairs.

We got off Lowestoft before noon and the ship was pointed between the piers. But they had not calculated the water at the entrance; consequence was she took the ground between the piers and there was a nasty jabble of a sea. She swung right across the mouth of the harbour and commenced to smash her bow and stern; she had a big overhung bow and stern.

Then the fun commenced. Hundreds of people flocked down to see the ship caught between the piers, the harbour master shouting out do this and the captain shouting do that, and all the time both ends of the ship were getting shorn off. Confusion supreme.

Eventually Lloyd's agent came down, seeing the condition of ship and crew, came on board with a gang from the shore. Ordered us all below and took charge. Took the ship into the harbour, when the tide made, and moored. This was on the Tuesday afternoon and right glad we of the crew were to get below and get food and rest after the two previous exciting days.

FROM this commences a new voyage. Our cargo was all discharged at Lowestoft and was sold there. Ship docked, stripped, caulked and recoppered, the masts hung on shearlegs, keel and keelson partly renewed, and what was of more importance, a new captain was appointed to the ship: Captain David Scott. He was the antipodes of Captain Mills. No whining or psalm singing about him; at least that was Jack's opinion and it turned out true. After being in Lowestoft over two months, we ballasted and left for Newcastle, there to load a cargo of coal for Shanghai, China. To the far East instead of far West, we had a fairly quick passage out without accident or incident. Fair strong monsoon in the China Sea. Stopping only a day at Anjar for water, we reached Shanghai later part of July [1860].

As far as I can recollect there were no coolies in those early days to work cargo on foreign ships. At least we got none and, dog days and all, the crew, only, discharged the whole coal cargo, the first half of which was dumped out. A trying job even in cold weather, but especially so in Shanghai during the dog days.

As far as I recollect, none of us got sick. We were all young, healthy men. The only water we had to drink was the water alongside, river water: a tub filled up every night and allowed to settle.

Shanghai was in its infancy. There was no part of the river bounded and all kind of filth was dumped in the river to mix with the water.

Our cargo was all out about August 20th. We got the ship cleaned down and ballast in about August 26th (the first day of the Dundee fair) so we got a month's wages and 24 hours liberty [to go ashore in Shanghai].

[*two*]

IN AND OUT
OF HAKODATE

OUR ship was chartered by Messrs. Dent & Co. of Shanghai for 18 months for the coasting trade and Japan trade. So about the 1st September 1860 we left Shanghai for Hakodate, the most northern [opened] port of Japan. At that time the port of Hakodate had been opened [since] about the year 1855 for American whalers to get fresh water and provisions, but there was no trade out of the port till the later part of '59. [The treaty opening Hakodate to vessels in need of supplies was concluded in 1854; commercial treaties followed in 1858.]

We had a very fine and fair passage up to the west entrance of Tsugaru Straits. Two islands lie off that entrance, 40 and 20 miles. It was here that our mate made a mistake for which he was afterwards discharged. He mistook the one for the other and altered the course, running the ship almost on a lee shore. He did this without calling or saying anything to the captain. After some twelve hours working to windward, we got in the straits and anchored at Hakodate about 3 o'clock afternoon in early September 1860.

Chinese we had seen and heard of before, but here we were among a quite different people both in dress and appearance. The first people to come on board were the customs officials, each wearing two long swords at his side. They brought a little wooden house with them; it was a little over six feet square. It was put up on deck for them to live in. The wood was all jointed and was put up in half an hour, roof and all. There was not a nail in the whole business. This held the two mats on which they squatted and slept at night. They had a box with a charcoal fire, which was used for making hot water for their tea in the daytime but was put out on deck at night when they slept. Everything about the house was neat and clean.

As we had to make our own way ashore, the boats were put out, myself and the oldest prentice appointed as crew; this in ordinary weather. I had a better chance than the rest of the crew of seeing the place and people and at that time they were a never-failing curiosity to us, as we were to them.

We boatmen did little or no work on the ship. After breakfast, we cleaned the boat to take the captain on shore. As a rule we were kept [on shore] waiting on him; but sometimes business took him on board to his meals. He was in great request on shore for the news he brought with him, as few ships came to Hakodate at that time—about one in two months.

At this time there were four foreign consuls in Hakodate: American, British, French and Russian. As I have said, in the season there were at times ten to twelve American whalers in Hakodate at once; the trading ships were British; and in the winter one or two Russian men-of-war dismantled their ships and wintered at the port.

Some French priests were the cause of the French consul being there at first. At least until five years later I never saw French ships in the port.

Hakodate itself, though one of the finest harbours in Japan, was a small place. All or most of the houses were built close to the sea. The junks used it as a port of call, coming up the coasts of the island for herring and salmon fishing.

As it was far away from the central government with a treacherous 20 miles wide strait between it and the main island and the only communication between was made by sculling boats when fine, by sail on the boats when fair wind, after the port was opened the central government ordered the *daimyo*, or princes, of Nambu and Tsugaru, the two northern principalites of the main island, to keep a certain number of their armed retainers in Hakodate to look after the foreigners. Besides there was the governor who lived in a fort outside the town. He had also a guard of two-sworded men. Any flunkey, cook or bottle-washer belonging to the above in either of the services wore a short sword, so that in the town two out of every three people wore one or two swords and would as soon leave his house without his head as [without] his sword. In fact, when the sworded men were about the streets, the people of the town kept to their houses, the women especially. There was no law for the common people against the two-sworded men. Seeing this was the case, all foreigners carried revolvers and besides always tried to keep a foreign ship in the harbour as a place of refuge to go to for themselves and families.

We loaded a cargo of peas and cedar boards. We were some six weeks in port before another foreign ship came in. Then we left for Shanghai. Arriving off Woosung, the mouth of Shanghai river, a compradore's boat came alongside, bringing letters and orders to take our cargo on to Hong Kong. Arriving there, were ordered to go to Whampao and discharge our cargo.

CHINESE are noted as expert thieves and even the veriest trifle is not too small for them to lift, especially anything brass or copper or what looked like either. They even stripped the copper off ships' bottoms, so whilst ships were at anchor at either Hong Kong or Whampao, besides the night watch, two boats had to be engaged to keep watch, one fastened to a rope at the jibboom end hung under the bow and one hung astern. We got off all clear.

After our cargo was out, we returned to Hong Kong. The chief mate was discharged there and 2nd mate promoted; an A.B. was shipped. There we loaded a general cargo of provisions of all kinds for Shanghai.

A few days before Christmas, the N.E. monsoon being at its greatest strength at that time, we worked up to windward, close to the China shore, anchoring sometimes at night, when the watch was doubled and had loaded muskets to scare away Chinese pirates. But we never came across any and when we got as far north as Cape Good Hope, we stood across the Formosa Channel for the south end of that island. Rounding it, we wrought up the east side of it. Here we had the Black or Japan Stream under our lee. Keeping in the stream till we were far enough north to fetch to windward of the Saddle Islands at the mouth of the Yangtsze river, we stood in for the river. When we got the river pilot on board, we had been only twenty days on the passage, which was considered a smart one for the season of the year.

Getting to Shanghai we found some of the opium hulks had moved up from Woosung to the lower reaches at Shanghai. After our cargo was out and ballast in, we were ordered to Chefoo to load. This passage was one of the roughest and coldest I have made. Arriving at Chefoo we found the harbour full of ice and had some trouble to get to the anchorage. It was some two days before we could land owing to the ice. At that time Chefoo Bluff was occupied by French soldiers. The only other foreigner we saw outside the French garrison was a Portague [Portuguese], the agent for Dent & Co.

TO get fresh beef at Chefoo the Captain bought a bullock, which came from some ten miles in the country. To turn the bullock into beef was the next thing. Among the crew was a Norwegian sailor, the only foreigner on board; he was shipped at Hong Kong when the mate was discharged. This man along with the ship's steward undertook to kill and dress the bullock.

The bullock was brought down to the beach by a Chinaman, led by a rope attached to a ring in its nose. Being the boatmen, we landed the 2 men and their tools, consisting of the carpenter's maul, various knives, etc. We lay off in the boat, waiting to take the beef on board and looked on.

The steward took the rope from the Chinaman. He left. The bullock stood quiet enough and the sailor struck it a heavy blow with the maul, which must have stunned it. But it did not fall, and the two men stood looking at it instead of following up the blow. A few minutes after, the bullock threw up his head, drew the rope out of the steward's hands, kicked up his heels, and started for his home in the country, the two men after it.

The steward came back soon, the sailor late at night. The next day the bullock was brought in again and the captain engaged the French soldiers to kill it, which they did in the most workman-like manner, their perquisites being the head, hide and feet for doing the killing.

⊰ 27 ⊱

WE loaded a full cargo of beancake at Chefoo. This we took to Shanghai and, as on the former voyage, at Woosung we got orders to take the cargo to Swatow or rather to Double Island, for Swatow was not open then; at least no foreign vessels had gone there. Our cargo out, we loaded a cargo of sugar, that is we filled up sugar but left a clear space of four feet right along the hold under the deck. This was filled up with Chinese coolies, as thick as they could stow, going to Shanghai, as to a land of promise, to get work.

It being the later part of April, we had rather a long passage and the coolies were getting short of dainties. One calm day, two sharks were swimming round the ship, and when the coolies saw them, they went nearly frantic. A shark hook was baited and put over, and after some coaxing one was hooked on. Then the coolies made a rush and [such] noise all had to be chased below, only the cooks being allowed to remain on deck. The shark, when we got it on board, turned out to be nearly ten feet long. After being killed, it was handed over to the cooks, less the back bone and head. After cutting off the fins and tail, the shark without any cleaning, was cut up, guts and everything going into the pot which was kept going all night.

Next day another shark was caught; it was also given to the coolies. On arrival at Shanghai the coolies left and we were glad to see the last of them. They left an awful mess behind them. However, the crew had nothing to do with the discharging of the cargo.

Cargo out, ballast in, as well as a lot of stores bought by the captain for sale at Hakodate, we left for that port. On this trip we had a passenger, Captain T. W. Blakiston of the Royal Artillery, famous for his survey of the upper Yangtsze river and his book thereon. On arriving in Hakodate in early summer [1861], we had fine weather.

This being our 2nd voyage to Hakodate, as I have said above, the Captain had bought at Shanghai a lot of stores on his own account for sale.

At that time invoices of cargo were not very particularly looked into; in fact, I don't think there was anyone capable of translating foreign invoices. Anyhow our long boat was put out and rigged, and as the *Eva* had three large stern windows which would let through gin or brandy and even larger cases such as Dawson's boot cases, after dark, when the hatches were closed, the crew got quietly into the hold through an opening made in the forecastle bulk head and carried the selected cases aft and through the bulk head to the cabin.

A man was detailed to keep the customs officers in their house on deck to see they did not come aft to look over the stern. This job fell to the mate. Chiefly a bottle or a little drop of rum or gin generally sent them to sleep.

The longboat, hauled close up under the stern, was quickly loaded and taken to a certain place on shore, close to the wall of the custom house which had been built out into the harbour. Plenty of help; the stores were quickly landed. In this way more than half our taxable stores were smuggled on shore every voyage we made to Hakodate. All free articles were landed in the regular way. To avoid suspicion when leaving the ship with smuggled goods, if the officers were around, we used to stand out the harbour with the boat; when far enough away we tacked and stood in shore. We never were caught.

It was well known that the merchants that came first to Japan, buying gold obangs [*ōban*] and kobangs [*koban*] all over the country, made piles of money; but it's probably not so well known that there was big money made by exporting copper cash and as their export was against the law, they had to be smuggled on board. What obangs or kobangs our captain bought, I don't know, but the quantity of cash we smuggled on board I know; as boatman I handled it all.

Cash that could be bought in Hakodate at this time at 4,200 for a dollar were sold in Shanghai at 1,200 or 1,300 for a dollar, and no freight was paid on them. So after landing our stores we would be taken to certain places by a guide and shown where the packages were hid, sometimes in a grave yard, and we backed them down to the boat. A single block on the spanker boom with a single rope rove through it and the cash were hauled up and taken through the stern windows: this was the routine for the next two voyages we made to Hakodate.

THIS time we loaded a cargo of sea produce, mostly seaweed, bêche-de-mer as well as dried shell fish, for Shanghai. Our passenger did not go back with us this trip as it was certain, barring accidents, we would be right back from Shanghai to Hakodate. So he waited over a voyage.

On arriving at the mouth of the Yangtsze we got into a typhoon. We got anchored just before it came down heavy, but we managed to ride it out without much damage. There was great havoc among native craft and at least one pilot boat was sunk, two foreign pilots and all her crew being lost. The Tungsha light ship was driven some miles away from her station. This we heard on arrival at Shanghai.

Our cargo out and ballast and lots of stores on board, we left for Hakodate.

In Hakodate there was the same work of getting stores ashore on the quiet and copper cash on board. We loaded same kind of cargo, mostly seaweed and other sea produce. While in Hakodate this time, we noticed the foreigners, at least some of them, when going outside their houses carried their revolvers at cock in their hands. Even Captain Scott, when he landed, took his pistol in his hand. It seems news had come up from Yokohama or Yedo that some foreigners had been cut down at the central ports.

I must say here that we two boatmen who were on shore at all hours of the night and day, our business sometimes taking us among grave yards and other lonely places, met all kinds of natives, even drunk two-sworded men, but were never molested by anyone.

WE got away on this our third voyage. It was beginning to get cold in early November. Got to Shanghai all right. Our cargo out and ballast in. This being our last voyage on the charter and as some Russian men-of-war were expected to winter in Hakodate, the captain bought an extra lot of stores at auction: beer porter and all kinds of liquor as well as eatables and some live sheep.

We left for Hakodate again, arriving there a few days before Christmas. We found two Russian men-of-war and two merchant vessels in port. The Russians had dismantled and housed-in their ships and, for the six weeks we were in port, the Russians had a merry time. They came on board and bought everything drinkable the captain would sell them, hoisting it up and taking it away in their own boats.

We loaded the same sort of cargo, seaweed principally, getting away last days of January [1862], taking two passengers with us: [a] Dent & Co. agent going on business and the American Consul Marshall who was going to join the Ever Victorious Army.

We had a quick passage. Strong N.W. winds all the way. Arriving at Shanghai early in February, our cargo was got out quick, the ship cleaned down, tea-ballast taken in. Topsides and decks caulked, the ship made ready to load a cargo of tea for New York. Freight £6. 10s. a ton.

We had a lively time at Shanghai. The Taiping rebellion was at its height. The Chinese were flocking into Shanghai from the country along both banks of the river for protection: a sad sight.

News of the Civil War in America had reached Shanghai, and I believe the affair of the stopping of the S/S *Trent* had also reached this port; news were anxiously awaited to see whether John Bull was not to take a hand in the fight. And as mail reached Shanghai only once in a month the steamer was anxiously looked for.

There was a play at the theatre and the house was crowded. In the middle of the play the steamer got in and the news was brought to the theatre that the *Trent* affair had been settled amicably. Then the crowd rushed out—they did not want any more play—shouting and singing, to hotel and club bars, acting like lunatics; they were happy. I happened to get a free ticket to the theatre that night and went along with the mate of our ship, and we were in the crowd.

Plate 2: A view of Hakodate harbor reproduced from a Japanese color woodcut of the late nineteenth century. (*Courtesy of the Municipal Library of Hakodate.*)

Americans mustered strong in Shanghai; three or four of the largest business houses in Shanghai were American.

AT THE beginning of April we finished loading our tea cargo and started for America. At this time of the year the N.E. monsoon was nearly finished and as we got south the winds got light and variable. We had a long passage down the sea to Anjar, where we got water and what fresh provisions were to be had.

Getting clear of Sunda Straits we soon got the S.E. trade wind and sailed merrily along till getting close to the south African coast, we encountered very bad weather. One day hail almost as large as hazel-nuts fell, and weather cold and stormy, heavy cross seas running. One day a heavy sea struck us on the beam ends while lying too. Caused the ship to spring a leak, which, in bad weather, kept us at the pumps more or less till we arrived at New York.

After rounding Cape of Good Hope we soon got into the the southeast trade winds and ran for St. Helena, where we anchored for fresh water and provisions. Left again same night.

I may mention here that as the Civil War in America was still going on, before leaving Shanghai we got orders to call at Halifax for orders, as Captain Symes and the *Alabama* were supposed to be cruising in the south Atlantic on the look-out for American ships from the Far East or vessels bound to the northern states with cargoes. When we arrived at Halifax, we found Mrs. Scott awaiting our arrival.

As expected, we got orders to go to New York with our cargo of tea. After getting fresh provisions on board we left

c

for New York, where we arrived early in October. Our Cargo discharged, ship was surveyed and caulked to try to stop the leak we sprung in rounding Cape Good Hope. We loaded a cargo of wheat in bags, on ship's account, for Dundee. Left New York first days of November.

HAD fair winds and moderate weather first few days, then the wind increased to heavy gale from S.W. Chopped round in a squall to N.W., causing heavy cross-sea coming up on both quarters.

One forenoon I was at the wheel and the captain was on the poop close beside me. Luckily no one else was on deck. Two heavy seas came on board one after the other and made a clean sweep of the decks; boats, bulwarks, galley, forecastle hatch—filling the cabin and forecastle with water.

All hands came rushing on deck. The forecastle hatch secured, sail was taken in, and the ship laid-to. Luckily also the hatch tarpaulins were intact. After everything was made as secure as possible, life lines were rigged along the decks from rigging to rigging so we could get along the decks. All hands went to the pumps; besides the water that came in from the seas that did the damage, we found she had sprung a leak again and from this time we had to stick at the pumps more or less till our arrival home.

After two days the wind and sea moderated and we were able to get the fore-hatch off, and we started to jettison cargo. Previously we had been jettisoning cargo from aft through the cabin and on to the poop, where it was washed overboard. So we had to take some from forward to keep the ship in trim.

After getting clear of as much cargo as was thought necessary, the wind being still fair and moderate, sail was made and the ship kept away on her course.

Again made Rockall, the Hebrides Islands. Got through the Pentland Firth on the East Coast of Scotland. Had very fine weather passing close to Aberdeen. Signaled to the town to telegraph to Dundee to send a tug boat to meet us.

Sailing along the coast we passed Montrose and, off Arbroath, we picked up the tug sent to meet us. We reached Dundee, anchored in the river on November 22, 1862, just 3 years to a day from the time we left it, November 22, 1859.

This completed my first nine years at sea.

[three]

TO OPEN AND
UNOPEN PORTS

HAVING been away for three years at one stretch, my people's, as well my own, inclinations were to stop on shore till spring. Going home one Saturday night, I met Captain Scott, who stopt me and said the owners had sold the *Eva* and were to build a new vessel better adapted for trading on the coasts of China and Japan. He also said that if I would pass an examination and get a certificate, he would give me a job as 2nd mate if I cared to go with him again.

So on Monday morning I went to the Navigation School and Friday the master told me I was fit to go up and pass. I went up before the examiners and passed all right, getting a mate's certificate.

Being engaged to go out to China and Japan in the new ship, I could not go far from home. So I shipped in a coasting collier in April [1863] as I got tired being idle so long. I shipped before the mast to go to Soham for coal, but when we got out the river we got an easterly gale and were driven up the Firth of Forth and while lying there wind-bound, the ship was chartered to load a cargo of coal at Granton for Boulogne. Then a strange thing happened.

Since that port was out of the coasting-trade limits, both captain and mate had to have foreign-going certificates. The captain had one but the mate had none. As I was the only other one on board who had a certificate, much against my will,

I had to go mate; and the mate took my place before the mast.

I made some four voyages in the coal trade, but got tired of coal dust, left and went up country for a month.

THE NEW SHIP was supposed to be launched in June, but the builders went bankrupt and the building was delayed. It was the middle of July before the ship was launched. Then she had to be rigged. I was taken on to superintend the work, and the middle of August saw her finished. We moved alongside a big crane to take in the boilers and machinery of the saw mill we were to take out to Hakodate.

On the 7th of September, two days before the Baxter Park in Dundee was opened, we left for Newcastle to fill up with coal. Leaving Newcastle, the later part of September, we had a fair passage to Anjar, where we got water and what fresh provisions were to be got. Left for Batavia; was there one day. Left for Samarang. There we discharged some 250 tons of coal. We were rather a long time over this, as we could only work up to 10 or 11 o'clock: owing to the monsoon freshing up and causing a nasty swell, the lighters could not lay along side. However, we got it out and left for Surabaja, where we filled up with rice for Hong Kong.

We had a long passage, having to go round east owing to the N.E. monsoon in the China Sea. Arrived at Hong Kong. Our rice out, we sailed for Hakodate direct, arriving there early in May 1864. There we discharged all the saw mill machinery and boilers and the balance of the Newcastle coal. Taking in a cargo of hardwood timber, we left for Shanghai, arriving there early in July.

The chief mate, who had been suffering for a long time from consumption and had been laid up all the passage from Hakodate, was taken to the French hospital on our arrival, and died in the hospital a week after he was taken there

It was very hot in the month of August that year at Shanghai and there were a lot of ships in port. Almost every morning one or the other of the ships had their flags halfmast; someone dead on board. We were over two months in Shanghai that time. Our cargo all out, we took in ballast and lots of stores, also five passengers, and left for Nagasaki.

FOR the next two years we traded between Hakodate and ports in China, from Chefoo in the north to Hong Kong and Whampoa in the south. At Hakodate we loaded square timber or planks after the saw mill got started.

The owners had three vessels in the east at this time: the bark *Akindo*, Captain Scott; the bark *Osuri*, Captain Paton; and the brigantine *Khankai*, Captain White. The manager of the company was Captain T. W. Blakiston, who resided at Hakodate.

IN the spring of 1867 we were at Shanghai and Captain Scott asked me to go to Hong Kong and pass an examination and get a master's certificate, but as H.M.S. *Rattler* was in Shanghai, it was arranged that I should take an examination, on board her, for navigation. Afterwards passing for seamanship before five of the masters of the tea clippers, I got through all right. Got a certificate.

In Shanghai this time Captain Scott bought an extra lot of stores of all kinds. Left Shanghai for Nagasaki. We were chartered to go to Kurume, an unopen port in the Gulf of Shimabara, there to load a cargo of rice for Osaka. After leaving Nagasaki, we hauled down the red ensign and hoisted the Japanese ensign and the Prince of Kurume's flag at the mast head : this we had to do. There [at Kurume] we loaded a cargo of Japanese rice for Osaka.

On our arrival at Osaka we found four different foreign fleets of warships and as many admirals; American, British, French and Dutch fleets, with an admiral in command of each.

After discharging our rice cargo at Osaka, we went to Hyōgo to take in ballast. When that was finished, the Japanese officials who had been on board since leaving Nagasaki hauled down their prince's flag as well as the Japanese ensign and went on shore. We hoisted the red ensign again and went back to Osaka to sell to the fleets the large quantity of stores we had brought from Shanghai.

As soon as the men-of-war people knew we had stores for sale, they came alongside in their boats and there was no trouble getting it out, as the men from the different ships hoisted or passed everything up themselves. Kobe [Hyōgo] was not opened as a port till the following year (1868).

From Osaka we sailed for Hakodate; loaded timber for China ports as before. In March 1868 we left Hakodate with a cargo of timber for Nagasaki, Amoy and Swatow. At Swatow we got clear of all our cargo and loaded a cargo of sugar for Shanghai, arriving at that port early in June.

There I had trouble with Captain Scott about the sailors breaking their leave. This was quite a common thing with our sailors in port, as the Captain give them money every Saturday while in port and they were supposed to turn up on Sunday night to be ready for work on Monday morning. But that was the exception. There were always some of the men more or less drunk or absent on Monday morning and the thing was getting too monotonous.

Many times I had asked Captain Scott to be less generous with money while there was so much work to do in port. This day two men had come on board the worse for liquor and had refused to turn out to work. At dinner time, while I was at dinner, they got into a sampan and went on shore. I informed Captain Scott what they had done and, at the same time, that either the two men or I would have to leave the ship.

Next morning I refused to let them turn to to work. They appealed to the captain and he came and told me to let them work. Thereupon I said I would refuse duty and went to my room. Of course, I was in the wrong, but I was getting so tired of the thing that I wanted to have it settled one way or the other.

Next day I was taken before the Assistant Judge, Mr. Mowat. When he had heard both sides, he summed up and told me it was hard on me, but I was in the wrong. I knew that, but I wanted the captain to know that after being 8 ½ years with him, 5 ½ as mate, there was a limit to my forbearance. Mr. Mowat looking at me said:

'You have had your trials and, from your looks, you seem to be a sensible man, but the law is against you and if you do not return to your duty and the captain insists on it, I must send you to jail for refusal of duty; I would be very sorry to have to do that.'

'I will go on board again,' I said, 'but I will do mate's duty only.' Hitherto I had done most of the pilot's work both in Shanghai and other ports but from that date would do mate's work only.

Two days afterwards the ship was ready for sea. She was lying in the upper reach of the river. The captain, when going on shore, told me to unmoor and drop her down below the shipping. This I refused to do and said he must either stop on board himself or send a pilot. This brought matters to a head. He saw I was to keep my word and as it was settled before the judge I was to do no more piloting, he consented to pay me off. I was very sorry to leave the old ship as I had seen her keel laid and was, outside the captain, the first man of her crew to be taken on.

AFTER BEING paid off, I tried to get 2nd mate in one of the river steamers, as I wanted to try steam after 13 ½ years of sail. But I had a friend in Shanghai who thought that instead of going 2nd mate I ought to get a command. And so, after I had been a week on shore, I received a note from the agents of the *Akindo*, the ship I had left, [which asked me to] call at Mackenzie & Co. and see Robert, who was head of Mackenzie & Co. I called and Mr. Mackenzie said:

'A friend of mine next door has a small ship for which he asked me to recommend a master; I thought of you—that you were just the man he wanted.'

We went in to see the owner and I was engaged out of hand. The vessel was a brigantine called the *Bob Tail Nag* and was lying at Nagasaki; I left for that port next day to join her.

When I got to Nagasaki I found the vessel was loaded with

general cargo, mostly tea bound to Tientsin. I also found her almost a wreck; amongst the rigging and running gear she had been badly looked after. In fact, she was so bad that had it not been for Mr. Maltby, the agent at Nagasaki, I would have refused to sail in her.

He told me he would pay for any gear I wanted; he also told me he had written to the owner about her condition.

Both the captain and mate were leaving, the captain to settle in Russia, the mate because a case of revolvers, worth $1,200, was short delivered.

I went to work and got rigging and rope and got everything fixed as well as could be done at Nagasaki. Wrote the owners at Shanghai to buy at that port gear that could not be got at Nagasaki and forward it to me at Tientsin. I shipped a mate and we got away from Nagasaki.

A week out off the Shantung promontory we got into a typhoon, not very heavy, but still heavy enough to do damage to vessels in the track of it. Our crew of eight Manila men and two Chinese, after sail was shortened and the ship laid to, with the exception of the boatswain, stowed themselves away below and would not come on deck. Luckily the only thing carried away was the port fore-lift, which I went aloft and secured myself.

On arrival at Taku, rounding to to come to anchor at Taku bar, the collar of the fore-stay was carried away. Luckily nearly all the sail was in, but had this happened during the typhoon, all our masts would have gone as it was the principal stay in the ship. In fact, not only the foremast but also the mainmast was dependent on it. The big main boom dropt on the taffrail when the stay went, but we got it lashed and set up again.

Pilots coming out, we got one on board, got over the bar into the river. Five vessels crossed at the same time, but there were only two river pilots available for the five ships, and as I had never been up the Peiho river before, I had either to go without a pilot or wait till one came back. This being my first command I wanted to get ahead. The pilot I had over the bar, who knew my experience in Shanghai river, said:

'You have a handy vessel and there are no banks in the middle; you will know from the look of the river banks which side is the deep water.'

He engaged a boat with four men for me, to run ropes ashore to check ship round the sharp bends of the river. Without a boat it's impossible even for a steamer to get to Tientsin. We were the first, of the five vessels that crossed the bar together, to get to Tientsin, beating the next ship by a tide, and he had a river pilot on board.

Our cargo turned out all right and in good order. Took some ballast in, and dropt down the river to Taku, where we took in our ballast, and left for Chefoo for orders.

At Chefoo we got the stores and gear from Shanghai that I had written for from Nagasaki, and we rove off the running gear we needed and put the vessel in good order. Then we got orders to go back to Nagasaki to load for Tientsin.

AGAIN at Nagasaki we loaded general cargo, again mostly tea and sea produce. Getting well on the fall of the year, we had strong head winds to beat against, but the *Bob Tail Nag* was a fast and handy vessel and we got along quicker than we expected.

Being November, it was getting cold in Tientsin. Got there, got our cargo out, dropt down to Taku to take our ballast in mud from the river bank, but this time it was frozen. We left for Chefoo again for orders. When we arrived at that port, we found our ballast was liquid and as we were ordered to Nagasaki again, I had the mud taken out and sand ballast put in before we sailed. I did not think it safe at that season of the year, especially as the mud ballast, as I have said, was frozen when taken in but had thawed in the ship.

At Nagasaki we loaded general cargo for Shanghai, mostly tea. There were three ships on the berth at the same time, loading the same cargo and bound for Shanghai: the bark *Serpent*, the barkentine *Norfolk*, and the brigantine *Bob Tail Nag*.

The *Serpent* got away first, five days ahead, then the *Norfolk* three days ahead. As there were no regular steamers at that time running between the ports, the last ship always carried mails, duplicate consigners' letters, etc. So when I was clearing out at our agent's office, the agents of the other vessels came in bringing their mails and letters and they started betting who would be the first of the three ships to arrive at Shanghai. Our agent said the *B.T.N.* [*Bob Tail Nag*] would not be the last for all the start the other two ships had, and he took a bet of $50 on it and looked at me. I said:

'The first has a five day start, the other a three day start; they are probably almost across by this time.'

'Never mind, I stand to my bet,' he said; 'the *B.T.N.* won't be the last of the three to get in.' He knew I had a fast and handy vessel and had had experience between the ports.

We got away and had strong, almost leading, winds. My experience told me to keep well north at that season of the year, so I steered to make the Amherst Rocks on the north side of the river entrance; after passing the rocks, making for the Tungsha light ship with a leading wind.

I saw the *Norfolk*, which had left three days before me, about eight miles due south of us and beating up to fetch the light-ship. Then I knew everything even [was all right]; I was at least a tide ahead of him. This was the 24th December 1868, morning. We got up as far as Woosung on that tide and with the next we got to Shanghai. I got on shore about 9 o'clock Christmas eve.

Called at the owner's house. He was not at home but was sent for and came. I delivered my letters and told him the story about the three ships and the race. Then he told me the *Serpent* had arrived that afternoon but was too late to enter at the custom house, so that the *B.T.N.* had really won the bet. Some two days afterwards the *Norfolk* got to Shanghai.

IN SETTLING my accounts with the owner at the end of the year, he refused to allow anything for pilotage. I had put in $300 for half pilotage, as it was the regular thing in them days if the captain did his own piloting. He offered $100, but I would not take it and was going to throw up the job.
Mr. Mackenzie was sent for and he persuaded the owner to give me $150 and asked me to stay with the ship. I said I would just then, as I had no other employment, but as soon as I got another chance I would leave her in any port she chanced to be at the time.

After getting some necessary repairs, we got away from Shanghai in the middle of January 1869 for Nagasaki seeking charter. When we got to Nagasaki, we found some six vessels seeking like ourselves.

There was one charter open, but as it was to an unopen port none of the other vessels would take it. So it came round to me. The agent called me to his office and explained the matter, saying it was a good freight and also saying that otherwise there was not likely to be any other freights going till after the Chinese New Year and the North China ports were opened.

The charter offered was to go to a place called Saga in the Gulf of Shimabara and take in a cargo of coal for Yokohama. I had been up the Shimabara Gulf while mate of the *Akindo*, loading a cargo of rice, so I saw no difficulty in the voyage; only they must supply a pilot to show me where to anchor. That settled, we left for Saga, and loaded a cargo of coal for Yokohama. It being winter time we had rather a rough passage, but, as I have said, the *B.T.N.* was not only a handy but also a fast vessel for her size. We got to Yokohama all right.

Our agents there had sold the cargo to the Pacific Mail Company, which had started a line of large, wooden, paddle-steamers between San Franscico and Hong Kong. They asked if I had any objection to taking the *B.T.N.* alongside the *America*, the steamer then in port; they would give me any help I wanted and the cargo would be discharged quicker. So I said all right, and the *B.T.N.* was put alongside.

While at Yokohama, I got a letter that had missed me at Shanghai and Nagasaki from my former employers, offering me the command of their schooner the *Khankai* with better pay than I had. . . . I thought this, outside of anything else, was my chance to get square with the owners of the *B.T.N.*; so while the cargo was being discharged, I told the agents that when the cargo was out, I was to leave and they had better look out for another master for the ship. There was like to be some trouble about finding another man and I saw the British consul and put the matter before him. They found a man and the matter was settled; I payed myself what was due me, and handed the command over. A week later I left Yokohama as a passenger in the *Khankai* for Hakodate. On our arrival there, I took over the command of her from Captain White on the 29th of March 1869.

Plate 3: Admiral Enomoto Buyō watching the Battle of Hakodate. Reproduced from a contemporary Japanese popular print. *(Courtesy of the Historiographical Institute of the University of Tokyo.)*

[four]

THE BATTLE
OF HAKODATE

THE CIVIL WAR was still raging in Japan, particularly at
Hakodate, which was still in the hands of the rebels, as they
were called at this time, and things were pretty hot. The Imperial troops were mustering at Aomori to attack them, and
the natives were in a quandary what to do. Without ships
they could not get away as the [pro-Tokugawa] rebels held
the surrounding country.

The *Khankai* was loaded with general cargo from Yokohama,
and I was ordered by the owner to take it across to Aomori and
land it there, one of the firm being over there. Lots of people
wanted to cross to Aomori to be out of the trouble that they
knew was brewing for the rebels at Hakodate. We had no
room for passengers and the authorities were very particular
about people leaving for Aomori, but one man, two women,
and five children managed to get smuggled on board and
pleaded to be taken to Aomori, telling me, if sent on shore
again, they would loose their heads. We got a head wind and
had to anchor in a bay for the night; the passengers were in
an awful fright for fear we would have to return to Hakodate.
But next morning we got [wind] aslant and got to Aomori
that afternoon. At Aomori we found the place full of two-
sworded fighting men, mustering to cross and attack the rebels
at Hakodate, but the imperial fleet and transports had not
arrived to carry them across.

+[49]+

D

Having so many soldiers in Aomori, the coolies thought they could treat foreigners with disdain in working out our cargo; they paid no attention to the officers and crew who were looking after the discharging. Told to be more careful and not break things, they got worse, collected together, and challenged the crew to fight. Hearing the row, I ran on deck. Seeing no other way to settle the matter, had the hatches put on, stopt the work, sent the coolies and boats on shore. Went on shore myself to see the agent. Told him the coolies had been breaking open boxes and tearing sugar bags and helping themselves to the contents. The officials, on being informed of this, had the men arrested, and as more or less of them had sugar or other parts of the cargo upon them, they were severely punished, and another lot sent off with an officer in charge of them to get the cargo out.

Cargo all out, we left for Tanabu in the northeast corner of the bay. There we loaded a cargo of house-building timber for Hakodate. When we reached Hakodate, we found things altered a good deal. The rebels were, however, concentrating on Hakodate, and the place looked as if the people were preparing for some great event. The authorities were more stringent looking after outgoing and incoming vessels. We got in and discharged our cargo and left again for Aomori, taking a few passengers with us. From Aomori we went once more to the north side of the bay and loaded timber again. This time we left a space clear in the main hatch, in which we put twenty bullocks.

When we got to Hakodate, we had some trouble with the officials before we could get in the harbour. This time all the foreign houses had their national flags flying over them, and the natives of the town were vacating their houses in the town and camping out on the hill. There was also a French corvette lying outside the harbour, standing by to take its nationals on board. When we left for Aomori again, American and British corvettes had arrived.

At Aomori we found that transports had been there and taken the Imperial troops away again. We went to Nambu. This time we only took in enough timber to make a level floor, then we took in some eighty cattle and left for Hakodate.

ON ARRIVING there, we found American, British, and French men-of-war all lying at anchor two miles off Hakodate; they had the Consuls and nationals of all countries on board.

As we were working up towards the harbour, the British man-of-war made a signal for us to anchor, which we did. They sent a boat and an officer on board and told us we could not go in the harbour, as all foreign vessels had been ordered out and the harbour was to be closed. But as we had live cattle on board and I found that Captain Blakiston, the owner, had not gone on board the man-of-war, I said I would go in far enough to open out the harbour [to get a clear view] and signal my owner for instructions what to do; which I did. Got orders to go as close to Nanai-hama as possible, hoist the catttle out and lower them in the sea; he was sending a boat and men to tow them on shore. This we did, and the cattle got on shore all right.

In the harbour were the only two men-of-war belonging to the rebels: an old paddle-frigate, formerly the *Eagle*, and the yacht *Emperor* which Queen Victoria had presented to the

Tycoon [the Shogun]. They were both in fighing trim, pre-
pared for action.

The next day we still lay at anchor close to Nanai-hama.
An imperial gunboat came round the head. She was a Dutch-
built vessel. She came right in and went into action at once,
and as we were in the line of fire, the British man-of-war sent
a boat and an officer and ordered us to shift out to where the
war vessels were at anchor. But before we got away, the
Emperor, which had come out to meet the imperial gunboat,
planted a shot in the imperial gunboat's magazine or boiler
and she blew up, so close to us that part of the debris came on
our deck. She sank at once: part of her crew went up and part
sank with the ship. A few men were left and they clambered
up the rigging of the foremast, which was standing half out
of the water. Some of the rebels on the beach started potting
at the men till the British man-of-war boats got between them
and picked the men up and took them away. From what had
occurred we found we were in a hot place and moved out at
once.

WHILE at anchor the next day a small paddle-steamer, called
the *Kaben-Dalem* under the Dutch Flag, came round the head,
and seeing the men-of-war all lying anchored outside, dropped
anchor alongside of us. Knowing me, [the captain] came on
board to see what was the matter. He was bound from Yokohama to Niigata and was short of coal. I told him no foreign
vessels were allowed in the harbour. He said he was going
in anyhow to see what he could do as he was under neutral
flag, i.e. there was no Dutch man-of-war around.

Two Hakodate residents who had been living on board the British man-of-war, on my arrival had asked permission to live on board my vessel while in port, thinking there was a better chance to get on shore from my ship than from the man-of-war. They wanted to get on shore to see after their house and property in the town. Here was a nice chance to get in the Dutch steamer and I also took the chance to get in and settle business with my owner, who had refused to leave his house and go on board a man-of-war when the consul and the rest of the British subjects left. So we all three got on board the Dutch steamer, and steamed in the harbour.

We got on shore all right. We had been an hour on shore when a letter from the authorities was handed to Captain Blakiston, my owner, in which they told him that my boat would be fired upon from the fort and stopped if it left the harbour for the ships outside; this meant I could not get back to my ship.

THAT NIGHT two more imperial war vessels had turned up. Both had been bought from the U.S. One was the famous ironclad *Stonewall Jackson*, the other the *Kaga no Kami*, a wooden gunboat built in America during the Civil War—one of the vessels that was said to have been built in ninety days. They came and had a look in the harbour, then went over to where the foreign men-of-war were anchored.

The *Eagle* and the *Emperor*, the two rebel ships we could see from the shore, were making great preparations for a fight. The *Eagle* was moored with her broadside onto the entrance of the harbour and all her guns were on that side of the ship; the *Emperor* was moored in the same way with all her guns trained on the harbour entrance.

At daylight next morning the two imperial vessels came in sight of the entrance and started bracing themselves for the fight. The first shot fired came from the big gun in the bow of the *Stonewall Jackson*—a 68 pound shell. It did not hit the mark by any means. A schooner was being built on the water front of Captain Blakiston's house; the shot struck the schooner, rebounded, struck the verandah of the house on the second storey; the doors being all open, it went clear through the sitting room. The boy was laying the cloth for breakfast in the dining room. The shot in its travels took the cloth off the table, went through the back of the house across the backyard, smashed into the cow's byre, and stopt there without hurting the cow, though she got a scare.

Seeing they were shooting so wide of the mark, I thought it was time to get up the mountain and said so to Captain Blakiston.

'Oh,' he said, 'hold on till we get our breakfast.—It will be all right to leave when they get the range.' Being an artillery officer he was used to that sort of thing.

But I could not see it and left to get my two friends Thompson and Bewick, who lived in the next compound but one from us, as they had come ashore with me.

In the intervening compound some 600 tons of Australian coal was piled up. While passing this pile, a shot from one of the ships dropt in the pile, scattering the coal close to me. This was too much, so I turned round and started for the mountain, my friends overtaking me before I had got far. When we got some 200 feet above sea level, a stray shot from some ship struck and carried away a corner of the French consul's house about ten yards ahead of us.

When we got up some 5 or 600 feet above sea level, we got among the townspeople camping on the hill and watching the naval battle in safety. From there they could see the effect of every shot.

They returned to their houses at night to sleep, as both sides quit fighting after dark. My friends and I also got to our houses to sleep and get something to eat during the lull. Next morning they started bright and early. I was still sleeping, but got up and into my clothes pretty quick, picked up some chow made ready the night before, and put for the hill again.

This day ended the naval battle in favour of the Imperialists. In the early part of the forenoon the *Stonewall Jackson* by mistake made a good shot with one of her 68 shells. She struck the *Eagle* just abaft the paddle wheels, making a hole large enough to drive a carriage and fair through. I also think some of her boilers must have burst. Anyhow, she sank at once, the crew making for the shore, some in boats from aft, most leaping over the bow and swimming.

Great jubilation on board the imperial ships, of which there were four, two more vessels having turned up during the night. They stopt firing for a spell, for what reason I don't know, probably expecting the *Emperor*, the only rebel vessel left, would haul down her flag and cave in. Anyhow, they had their dinner quietly. Since the *Emperor's* flag was still flying in the afternoon, they closed in upon her and riddled her with shot; from small guns, I think. What we saw was the *Emperor* getting into shallow water and settling down, the crew getting overboard and swimming on shore. So ended the naval battle of Hakodate.

All this time the fort at the mouth of the harbour had not taken any hand in the fighting; there were guns enough on the fort but I think no shot or shell.

The naval battle finished, most of the townfolk returned to their houses and shops; a few were opened. Most of the men from the sunken ships got into the fort and as they seemed to have rifles and ammunition, they started shooting promiscuously to the great danger of people walking about the town on business or otherwise.

The Governor's residence, called *Goryōkaku*, a mile from Hakodate as the crow flies, was a kind of small fort with a deep moat all round it, and it was supposed the rebel leaders were hanging around there. The *Kaga no Kami* came into the harbour and moored with her broadside facing the *Goryōkaku* fort, the outlook of which could be seen from the harbour. She started firing at the *Goryōkaku*, planting her shot, as far as could be seen, in the neighbourhood of the fort and one lucky shot struck the outlook. As far as I can remember, that settled the matter.

The Imperialists landed a lot of men during the night outside the harbour. Their men climbed the back of the hill, came over the top and down inside to the town, thus taking the rebels in the rear. Other Imperial troops had been landed at several places along the coast and had driven the rebels from the country on to the peninsula and got them between two fires. After a little fighting the rebels caved in; this ended the war of the restoration of the Mikado.

I may mention here that the rebels—*dassō* [脱走] the Japanese called them—had all done away with their top knots; their hair had been allowed to grow long and was cut round in foreign style. A lot of the rank and file were kept here as prisoners and turned out every day to cut down and level part of the hill to make a large square piece of level ground on which was built a shrine, called the *Shōkon-sha* [招魂社]. Every year since, they have a two day holiday at the *Shōkon-sha* on the anniversary of the end of the Civil War.

[*five*]

TO SAGHALIEN
AND VLADIVOSTOK

WITH THE WAR FINISHED, the trade to Aomori Bay was also finished, and in September we were sent to Kushiro, an open harbour on the east coast. There we loaded a cargo of seaweed and brought it to Hakodate. Having had a rough voyage, our vessel started to leak badly. (Since she had run on a reef a year previously, nothing had been done to her bottom.) We were loaded with a cargo of wood and sent to Shanghai for docking and repairs.

While in Shanghai, H.M.S. *Galatea*, captained by the Duke of Edinburgh, arrived and anchored outside Woosung in the main river. They had come from Australia. While in that country, some Irishman fired a shot at the duke, but missed him. When I saw him on the race course in Shanghai, he seemed to have a scared look on his face and was always looking round about him as if on watch.

AFTER getting our repairs done, we took in stores and left for Hakodate via Nagasaki. At that port we met the *Akindo*, Captain Scott [commanding]. She had just arrived from Hakodate and brought the news that rice was scarce and dear at that port. So we got orders to load a full cargo of rice and get to Hakodate with it as soon as possible. With all dispatch we were loaded and got away.

When we got to Hakodate, we found that rice was so scarce and dear that poor people could not afford to buy it and were living chiefly on potatoes and the roots of the common bracken fern, which grew plentiful on the tablelands in the locality. Our cargo was soon landed. A great amount of cod had come on the coasts of the strait so we took in some ballast and went to several villages in the strait to load cod fish for Yokohama. Some fish previously caught and salted was put on board from the shore and the boats came alongside with their fresh catch which was salted in the hold. At the village of Todohoki, north of Cape Esan, we got most of our cargo and when finished there we left for Yokohama.

We were some time getting clear of our cargo. When finished, the agents Messers. Grauert put on board lots of stores and other Japanese cargo, and we left again for Hakodate. We had a long rough passage up and were kept in port some time.

WE were chartered by the government to take emigrants and stores to Saghalien. The Japanese at that time claimed the southern part of that island, and Kushunkotan in Aniwa Bay was the official headquarters. About the end of May, we got away with some 120 emigrants and a cargo of rice and other native food. At that season the winds were variable, mostly light east with drizzling rain or fog, which was not pleasant for passengers nor crew.

In La Pérouse Strait [Sōya Kaikyō] a passenger died from stricture and as I saw no chance of us reaching port for a couple of days or more, I proposed a burial at sea. When the passengers heard of this, they set up a howl, and said they would not allow it. They tried force at first, but after a little reasoning with them they quieted down and allowed the burial to take place.

The next day we arrived at Kushinkutan. As soon as we were anchored, the Japanese officials came on board to get letters and see the immigrants; they were a sorry looking lot; looked more like exiles than colonists. However, they soon had our passengers on shore which allowed us to get the ship washed down, which we had not been able to do all the passage.

At this time the Russian and Japanese settlements at Kushunkotan were within less than a mile of each other, a spur of a a hill about 200 feet high between them. A Russian colonel was in charge of their settlement and had under him probably 200 men and a doctor to attend them. The Japanese settlement had only civil officials. Both peoples seemed to hob-nob together and be good friends.

As we were the first vessel to reach the place that year, everyone that could get on board came to see if we had anything to sell. As our cargo was government stores, I had been advised by friends in Hakodate who knew the business to buy and take up for sale all kinds of drinkables and eatables such as sugar and flour.

As it happened, there had been a small vessel in Hakodate from Hong Kong. Someone there had gone into a speculation, bought up anything that was unsalable in the auction rooms at Hong Kong, chartered this vessel and sent her to call at all the ports in Japan. After calling at Kobe and Yokohama, selling all they could, they came to Hakodate with the balance. I had bought two or three casks of spirits, some cases called champagne, some cases of brandy and gin, beer and porter, and a miscellaneous lot including some six gross of finger rings with stones; this had been a cheap lot at $2 a gross.

As soon as the Russian officers heard there was liquor for sale, the colonel came on board and sampled it and would have taken the whole lot at my price. He got the lion's share, but I kept some for the rank and file. The native Ainu men and women bought all the rings and gewgaws. Here again the first comers wanted to buy the lot, but I said:

'No, give others a chance.'

However, we sold all out, as well as all the ship's stores we could spare; and pleased they were to get them at the price.

We lay at Kushunkotan for three weeks. During that time the beach was littered with some thousands of pressed cubes of herrings, the stench from which is bad enough at any time but either from the want of labour or owing to the foggy drizzly weather, the stuff had become putrid. The officials seemed to have made no preparations for the immigrants we took up. The little gully where the settlement was was half swamp or bog, and they erected board and mat shacks for the people to live in *pro tem*. The stink from accumulated secretions and the putrid herring on the beach caused a malaria, and a third of the people we landed were either sick or died during the three weeks we lay there.

Unfortunately our crew also got sick and I got the army doctor from the Russian settlement to attend to them. At one time six out of the crew of ten were laid up. The Russian doctor said it was not a deadly disease, that as soon as we got to sea the men would recover. This was true so far, but our boatswain never recovered and died on our arrival in Hakodate.

Our return cargo was repatriated invalids. They covered the single ballast with straw mats and enough bedding to make a soft bed, then they brought some eighty sick alongside. One dozen were able to get up with help, but more than half had to be hoisted on board and lowered in the hold by tackle. They were all in two rows, their feet to the ship's side and their heads towards midships; this left a clear space between the rows of six or eight feet for the doctor and attendants to look after them.

Before leaving, I told the governor about the trouble we had to get the man that died on the way up buried at sea. He said he had given instructions to the doctor that if anyone died, they were to be buried at sea if so ordered by me. Besides the sick, we had about fifty women and children belonging to them, all glad to be going back to Japan: a sickly, dirty lot they looked.

We had a fine and quick passage to Hakodate. No one died before our arrival, but for some reason they kept them for two days on board after we arrived, and two died in the interval. My mate, who had caught the malaria pretty bad, I had to leave behind; the boatswain died in the hospital the day after our arrival.

AFTER a couple of weeks in Hakodate, we were again chartered by the Japanese government to take provisions and a few officials to Kushunkotan and on our return trip to call at Sōya, the extreme north settlement of Yesso Island [Hokkaido].

In the autumn of 1868, H.B.M.'s corvette *Rattler* had been

wrecked while surveying the large Sōya Bay in La Pérouse Strait. The guns, provisions and all the movable gear belonging to the vessel were landed by her crew on the beach at Soya village, stores and perishable goods being put under cover.

In the autumn of 1869 Captain Blakiston started from Nemuro, where he had landed from the *Akindo*, traveled up the east coast of the island, crossed the Shiretoko Peninsula, all along the N.E. coast, till he arrived at the north point: Sōya village. There, he surveyed the guns and gear landed from the *Rattler* and reported to the officials. I may mention here that everything salved and unsalved from the *Rattler* was gifted to the Japanese Government.

The French corvette *Duplex* went to Sōya and carried the officers and crew of the *Rattler* to Yokohama.

On Captain Blakiston's report reaching the central authorities at Tokyo, they ordered the guns of the *Rattler* brought to Tokyo and ordered the Hakodate officials to make arrangements for their transport. They [in turn] contracted with Captain Blakiston for the transport. Besides the freight on the stores to Kushunkotan, he was to receive 3,000 Rios and all the provisions and gear salvaged from the *Rattler*, as well as all we could get out of the wreck or from the bottom of the sea, for taking the guns to Tokyo.

The *Rattler* was a wooden, ship-rigged sailing vessel with an auxiliary screw which could be lifted up out of the water when under sail and lowered down when steam was used. As the old wooden walls of England were built of oak and fastened with pure copper bolts right through and Captain Blakiston had reported that both sides and the bow of the *Rattler* were lying high on a rocky ledge close on the beach, it was settled we should take twelve Japanese carpenters with their tools (they could also be used as labourers); we also took some cases of coal oil to burn the woodwork.

We got away from Hakodate and had a fine, quick passage to Kushunkotan, landed our cargo and the few officials we had, and left for Sōya. There we found a break in the ledge of rocks that ran round the bay. Inside we found a small bay, clear of rocks, just large enough for our small ship, where we could lie with safety in any wind protected from the northwest by a ledge that rose to within six feet of sea level, just a natural little harbour within a mile of the wreck and fairly teaming with edible fish. When the wind blew off the land east or southeast, it would blow the water out of the harbour and make a difference of six feet; when blowing from west or northwest it would raise the water above the normal.

We got into this little bay all right. There we found the crew of the *Rattler* had landed everything salvaged from the wreck—guns, anchors, chains, cables, hawsers, spars, yards, etc. All perishable goods on the beach, sails, furniture and stores as well as all ropes and spare gear had been carried up and put under cover, well protected.

From Hakodate we had a customs officer to deal with the official at Sōya and as he had no other duties to perform he and the cook's mate were told to keep the ship supplied with fresh fish. Captain Blakiston's partner, Mr. Marr, also went with us as interpreter.

After making the ship safe, Mr. Marr, the head carpenter, and myself [went ashore]. The customs officer had landed the night before, and as we landed he met us on the beach with the village people. They took us around and showed us where all

E

the stores etc. were stored. This took up the greater part of a day.

When we got back on board, I put my plan of work before Mr. Marr and asked his opinion. He said he had only come as interpreter, that the work was intrusted to me and he was sure it would be well done; this left me a free hand.

We started in. When the weather was bad or rough, we wrought at and got on board the gear. Salvaged the guns, anchors, cables, provisions (beef and pork in barrels) and all the furniture (mahogany extension dining table, chairs) and a large, well-stocked medicine chest, etc. etc.

Gear for lifting and taking on board we found plenty, all ready rove; only had to stretch and make fast the end of the spars to the masts. We found all kinds of purchases ready rove, light or heavy, and the ropes and blocks in good order. The guns, as far as I recollect, were sixty pounders and among them were six breech-loader Armstrong Guns; this was the first time I had seen breech-loaders.

At the wreck, in fine weather, we also got a lot of pure copper, brass, and gun metal of which the propeller was made. We found the latter and all the boilers and machinery lying in five fathoms of water in the trap in which the ship was caught. My Japanese sailors and carpenters made no bones about going down in three to five fathoms and putting a strop on a shaft, then hooking a tackle. In early September the weather was warm and the water clear . . . and all hands seemed to enjoy and take great interest in the work; in fact, I had to restrain them at times, as they wanted to pick up anything that looked like brass or copper, but our ship was getting full and I did not want what was of small value, such as powder boxes which were strewn about. A few we lifted after a great deal of trouble and though there were lots more about, we considered they were not worth spending time over.

Our hold was full, and on our deck we took three of the four boats. Left behind the launch (not a steam one) as it was too large to put on deck. But we used it all the time at Sōya for carrying the guns, anchors, cables and all the heavy gear. With it and two fishing boats we lifted the propeller and shafting out of the sea. Thus we spent six weeks wrecking the *Rattler*, hard but pleasant work.

Upon arrival at Hakodate, we were ordered to trans-ship all the guns, anchors, cables and other heavy gear to the *Akindo*, which was to carry them to Yokohama. She got away from Hakodate the beginning of October and on the 11th of October 1870 got into heavy typhoon and was totally wrecked in Odawara Bay, the guns this time going down with the ship. The Japanese goverment went to the expense of sending divers down and lifting the guns and eventually got them to Tokyo, but most of the gear of the *Rattler*, put on board of the *Akindo*, was not recovered.

AFTER lying in Hakodate for some time, we were chartered to take emigrants to Nemuro, which at this time was coming into prominence as the place to make a town, mostly due to the influence of Mr. Yanagita Tokichi, known by his mark ㊉ *Maruhon*, who had got some fishing rights on the Nishibetsu river, some 20 miles from Nemuro.

Among the settler passengers was the whole of the inmates of a *jorōya* [whore house], who were going to start business there. If I remember right, this was the first house in that line of business to start east of Hakodate. We carried their houses as well as the people.

After getting rid of our cargo and passengers, we left for Nishibetsu river to load salmon. As it was November—the season for that fish—we had no trouble lying off the coast. We got about 120 tons on board, then left for Nemuro again, where we got in some more. Then we had to wait till the fishermen got to Nemuro from Nishibetsu and other rivers. Mats having been put on top of the fish, some 150 fishermen came on board to be taken to Hakodate.

It being well on in November, we had the regular westerly winter winds against us, but our vessel was both well found and well manned and we managed to get along fairly well. We had to anchor for two days under lee of Cape Yerimo; when we got as far as Cape Esan, we got the full force of the current running through the strait. As we could not get to an anchorage on the north side of the strait, our water and wood getting short, we stood across the straits, fetched into the bay west of Shiriyasaki, and making short tacks off the south shore, wrought as far as the large village of Obata just before dark, and anchored off the mouth of a small river. People came off from the shore and an agreement was made with them to bring wood and water the next day.

As many of the fishermen belonged to the district around Obata, they asked and got permission to leave the ship, saying that if they went to Hakodate they would have to take a ship and come back again. As there was a man belonging to the charterers on board, I left it with him to settle the matter. In this, I later found, I did wrong as all the men should have been taken to Hakodate first to be settled.

With wood and water on board, we left Obata with a tide running west. They told us to make short tacks off the south shore: the tide would help us as far as the Singapore rock. Getting as far as the cape, found the current of it like a mill stream. Stood out heading for the east side of Hakodate-head, but as soon as we got in the strait current, we were swept away eastward and barely fetched Shiokubi-head. Seeing some junks lying at anchor off a small village and bay called Shiura, kept away and came to anchor between them.

Found out we had got to the regular wind-bound anchorage for junks, lying in wait for a chance to get to Hakodate during the winter winds. Though it was blowing strong from W.N. W., we lay quite snug and got no sea. Next morning, as there seemed no chance of change of wind, all the passengers, with one or two exceptions, said if we would land them, they would walk to Hakodate. So before noon they were all landed, and, taking some food with them, they started for Hakodate.

After turning in that night, the wind fell away and hauled to the south. The junks began to get in their anchors. Got all hands on deck and got underway. The wind just lasted long enough; we managed to crawl into Hakodate when it came away from the northwest again fresh. A few of the junks managed to get in, some anchored east of the head, and some had to go back again. Our passengers were much surprised next morning, when they found the vessel had got into Hakodate so soon. We found three barks flying German flags; they had come in for fear of French men-of-war.

We got in some more cargo after lying some time in Hakodate, and left for Yokohama. While in Hakodate, letters had come from Otaru that the people at that place were short of

rice and as there were no French men-of-war so far north, the
captains of the German ships were asked if any of them would
go, but they all refused, not so much [out of] fear of the
French, as of the weather and the voyage. We had rough passage down, spent Christmas and New Year [1871] at sea.
On arrival at Yokohama, we soon got our cargo out and stores
and some cargo in; we left again for Hakodate. After a long,
rough passage, we arrived about the end of February. In the
harbour were still lying the three German barks.

AS SOON as we got anchored, Captain Blakiston, the owner,
came on board, and told me the people at Otaru were in great
straits for rice, and asked me if I would try to get a cargo of
rice to Otaru. I said, certainly; then with all dispatch our cargo
taken out and rice loaded, we left for Otaru. We had a rough
but fair passage till we got to within 12 miles off Otaru. In
fact, two miles further would have put us in a position of
safety, but there being no wind and a heavy northerly swell
setting us on the shore, we had to anchor about half a mile off
the bold headland rising some 800 feet. Before we got the
sails well fast, the north gale that the swell foretold was upon
us, and all hands thought that that was the last day of the ship
and ourselves.

But we had reckoned without the high bluff land. We had
got both anchors down and the stream-anchor with a seven
inch new Manila hawser on it, everything battened down, and
gear on deck lashed secure, when the thing we never thought
of happened. The north gale came on and blew hard with heavy
breaking sea, but the wind blowing against the steep bluff

under which we were lying rebounded and we were lying almost in a calm, broadside onto the heavy sea. Rolling so no one could stop on deck and enough to take the masts out of her, things looked pretty bad. At the very height of the gale she never rode to her anchors. Lots of people collected on shore to watch. It turned out, they knew we were loaded with rice for them, and stood expecting every minute we would be driven on shore.

But northerns on the coast of Hokkaido never last long. Next morning it was calm, but still a swell on. We got in two anchors and, some boats coming to our help, we got the third anchor. The boats taking us in tow, we got round the corner, and a breeze coming away, we got to Otaru, where our cargo of rice was quickly taken out. After ballasting, we left again for Hakodate.

DURING the time we were away at Otaru, the government offered another charter to take a cargo of coal from the Kayanuma Coal Mine to Futami on Sado Island for the gold mine at Aikawa. One of the German barks that were war-bound took the charter and got to Kayanuma all right and anchored off the mouth of the ravine where the coal was lying. The captain got on shore early in the morning and made arrangement for getting the coal off.

The anchorage was open to winds from south round west to N. W. He had just got back on board his ship, when a W. S. W. gale suddenly sprung up, and his anchors dragging, his vessel struck a rock lying some 60 fathoms off the shore, slewed broadside onto sea and wind, and broke all to pieces; all hands were drowned.

The news of the catastrophe reached Hakodate some few days before we got there from Otaru; cast quite a gloom over the place. But the coal was wanted at Sado Island; so the officials came to our owner again asking if he would let the *Khankai* go. As we had done the Otaru trip a month earlier in the season, they thought we could manage where others failed. I was called and asked if I would undertake the job. I said:

'If you risk your ship, I take the risk.'

We had a fine and fair passage up, anchored off the place early in the morning. After breakfast went on shore to see the head official. He took me up the ravine to the mine, and showed me all the workings in the mine. When we came out and were coming down facing the sea, we found it was blowing a gale on shore. Hurried down to the beach. Found the ship with all her chain and three anchors down, going almost bows under to the heavy seas as they came along. This within three weeks of the wreck of the German at the same place. It looked fearsome from the shore for some two hours, till in the afternoon the wind began to take off as quick as it had risen, and by sundown it was almost calm.

Looking along the shore, I found an inlet between some rocks, large enough to hold three or four junks. As it was too early for the junks to come north, I thought it would hold the *Khankai*. There were also heavy posts in the rocks for making ropes fast. So I told the official I would take the vessel in there and he would have to send the coal to that place, some half mile away from where she was at anchor. Next morning being fine, the [Japanese] sent boats and towed us along and moored us. There was only one house at the place; it was called Chatsunai [the MS states Chats]. Although we had one or two blows with heavy sea, the ship was safe.

We got loaded and got to Sado all right. We anchored in the south bay, at a place called Futami. Got our coal out and ballast in; told to go back to Kainuma for another cargo of coal. We made all together three trips to Sado with coal; got back to Hakodate, made a voyage to Nemuro, back to Hakodate. Lay some time.

LOADED a full cargo of seaweed and left for Yokohama [1872], where our cargo was trans-shipped on board the British Steamer *Duna*, afterwards bought by the Japanese and called the *Suminoya Maru*. She took the seaweed to China.

As the owner, Captain Blakiston, was a passenger with us this trip and wanted to go through the Inland Sea, we took on board stores and left for Kobe. We had a long passage beating the winter westerly gales. We anchored in Oshima for five or six days; weather moderating, we left. But before we got to the entrance of the Kii Channel, it began to blow heavily from the northwest. We ran into a small harbor, where we lay three days, and our owner got some good shooting. Eventually we got an easterly wind and reached Kobe, where we got some turbines and other machinery for Sado gold mines, filling up also with coal for the mines.

As I have said, the owner, Captain Blakiston, was on board. While at Kobe, H.M. surveying vessel the *Serpent*, under Commander Bullock, was there, and as Captain Blakiston and he were old friends and she was then engaged correcting former surveys from the *Serpent*, we got all the latest chart corrections for the Inland Sea. So it was settled we should make our way through the sea to Shimonoseki, being among the first, if not the first, foreign sailing vessel, to go right through the sea (January 1872).

As Captain Blakiston himself had some eleven years previously surveyed and charted the upper Yangtsze River, we wanted no pilot; it was our intention not to stick exactly to the track laid down on the chart but to work our way through the islands wherever the wind would let us. As we were in no hurry, we made it a pleasure trip, anchoring off some of the islands for a day or two sometimes. When we reached Shimonoseki we anchored off the town for three days, Captain Blakiston going on shore shooting at all the places. It was the middle of February before we got to Sado Island, where we stayed a couple of weeks with Mr. Gower and Mr. Scott.

The middle of March, got back to Hakodate, where we stayed some time. Loaded a cargo for Shanghai. On our arrival at that port found our agents had been instructed by our owners to buy a small steamer for Hakodate. After looking at two or three for sale, it was decided to buy the *Maggie Lauder*. She had originally been built for the Confederate States, but never left Birken-head, where she had lain for years, and had been bought cheap by a shipmaster who had been in the East; she had been taken out round the cape to Shanghai and put on the river as a tug boat, but was found to be too big and unhandy. Our people got her cheap, as there were some alterations to be made on her for the long passage to Hakodate.

I was ordered by letter to leave my mate behind to bring her to Hakodate and take in stores at Shanghai, get to Nagasaki fill up with coal and go to Vladivostok and sell what I could. I was recommended by Mr. Wilson of Lane Crawford & Co., Shanghai, to appoint Mr. G. Denbigh at Vladivostok as my agent. He managed to sell all the stores but could do nothing with coal.

At that time Vladivostok had only about fifty houses all told, including government and telegraph buildings. In fact, stores and merchants were more than half the people in the place. Who they did business with, I don't know; people from the country round about, I suppose. Some six years later they shifted the capital from Nikolaevsk to Vladivostok; the rush was made to that port. Anyhow, in 1872, when I was at Vladivostok, there were no roads, just footpaths, to the houses.

six

THE AOMORI
TO HAKODATE RUN

NOT BEING ABLE to sell the coal, brought it to Hakodate and discharged it on arrival. The steamer *Maggie Lauder*, bought at Shanghai, had arrived and was lying there, and I was asked to shift my traps on board of her and take charge of her: my former mate, who had brought her from Shanghai, relieving me in the schooner.

The steamer had been put under the American flag when she left Shanghai. We lay some time in Hakodate waiting for the Japanese to find the money to take her over, and get a Japanese flag for her. But as they were a long time about it, we made, with government consent, several voyages coastwise to Otaru and Muroran.

Our first trip to Aomori [1873], we were full of passengers. I had landed to make arrangements with the agent there, when the boatman called my attention to the steamer. When I looked, there were Japanese soldiers dressed in hussar uniforms crowding on board. On making inquiries, I found the soldiers had been waiting on board two junks to sail for Hakodate. The second son of the czar of Russia was expected at Hakodate, and the hussars were to act as his body guard, so I had to get on board at once and return to Hakodate.

The next day a Russian man-of-war arrived with the prince on board. As far as I recollect, he was three days in Hakodate.

They kept our steamer waiting to take the escort of hussars back to Aomori, some four days all together.

We made two or three more trips to Aomori, bringing across coolies for the herring fishing. When that was finished, a man in Hakodate made a contract with the Kaitakushi [Hokkaido Development Commission] officials to supply 150,000 *koku* of house-building timber from Nambu and Tsugaru, the timber to be landed at Otaru and Muroran, so much at each place. Junks were chartered to do the carrying and the contract time was three months to finish the landing at the above ports. They chartered the *Maggie Lauder* to do the whipping up [loading, probably owing to lack of wharf facilities], and they made me commodore of the fleet since most of the timber had to go to Otaru and the junks after leaving Aomori bay had to be towed some fifty miles to the westward before they were clear of the intake of the current through the straits.

They were all towed out. All the junks being supplied with a distinguishing flag so they could call the steamer and that we should know them among other junks, the contract was finished in time.

About this time they managed to get the steamer transferred to some Japanese and her flag was changed as well as her name to *Meishin Maru;* we were to run between Aomori and Hakodate. They advertised all down the west coast of Nippon as far as Niigata and down the east coast as far as Sendai, that the steamer would leave Aomori for Hakodate every fourth day, this starting the first steam passenger traffic across Tsugaru Strait.

Summer was the slack time for coolies crossing and at first

therc were not many passengers, while the mails were [being]
sent across from the nearest point to Hakodate. But after we
had been two months running, passengers began to come, as
well as the mails.

THE *Khankai* ran high and dry on shore at Chatsunai, where
she had gone to load coal for the gold mines at Sado. We were
sent up to see what was the matter, and to get her afloat if
possible and bring her to Hakodate. We found her ten feet
above the water on a pebbly beach, nothing much the matter
with her only some copper off her bottom and planks chafed in
some places.

The captain and crew had done nothing, waiting for orders
from Hakodate. So I started them sending down sails and
striking the masts; then headed for the coal mine to interview
the officials to help me get coolies to discharge the ballast over
the side on the beach. When I had got half way to Kayanuma
I met a party who were coming to see me. One was a Dutch
gentleman I had met in Yokohama; his companion was the
famous Admiral Enomoto [Takeaki], who was travelling
through Hokkaido inspecting mines, etc.

After some talk the admiral asked me what was to be done
about the *Khankai*, and I told him what I intended to do and
that I was on my way to see the officer at the mines to ask his
help in getting coolies. The admiral gave me to understand
that he at that time was the superior officer and he would give
all the help, both in men and material, they could supply from
the mines. He sent word by one of his men to the mining
officer, and I turned back with him to the ship to see about
what we would need in the way of material and to consult with

Mr. Thompson, the ship builder who had come with me from
Hakodate to help get the *Khankai* afloat.

After consultation, we agreed upon a plan to take all the
ballast out, strike everything to the lower masts, and shore up
the lower masts with spars. The vessel was lying canted away
from the sea; canted shorewards. Tackles were rove from her
mast heads and others, fast to the rocks. After everything was
cleared out of the vessel, the ends of the tackles were taken on
board the steamer, and she turned over quite easily on beds
that we had made.

The beach was composed of large, clean shingle with a grade
of about a foot in three; this we helped by clearing away the
shingle under the bilge on the side next the water, so she
would be easier pulled into the sea. Getting her two cable
chains on board the steamer and securely fastened to the steamer's mainmast, we went ahead slow, and the simple tighten-
ing of the cables the first time jerked the *Khankai* down and
round some feet.

But simply keeping the chains tight and going full speed
had no effect so we carried out the first manœuver [i.e. jerking
the cables] till we got half of her afloat. Seeing we had her in
hand and it being a dark night and windy-looking, we let her
lie all night. The next morning after one hour's towing, we
had her afloat.

That morning Admiral Enomoto came early, bringing a lot
of men and boats to put the gear and stores on board that had
been put on shore. By 3 p.m. everything was finished. He
even offered to give me coal enough, gratis, to take us to Hakodate. As we had coal enough, I thanked him, as I wanted to
get away as quick as possible; the people in Aomori would be

ブレキストン線發見者
〈動物分界線トシテノ津軽海峡〉
函館在留英國人
デ.タブリュー.ブレキストン
所有船

Plate 4: One of the sailing vessels belonging to the Blakiston Line. *(Courtesy of the Municipal Library of Hakodate.)*

wondering where the mail and passenger steamer had got. This was in pre-telegraph days.

WE missed only one trip across the straits. For about eight months [in 1874] we did well, the passengers increasing, and there was always plenty of cargo from Aomori. Things looked flourishing. Then the Japanese government officials got jealous. Knowing the *Meishin Maru* was partly, if not all together, foreign owned, they thought they ought to have a share.

Count Kuroda, at that time head of the Kaitakushi, had a down on foreigners, especially Britishers, from the way they treated him on board a British man-of-war after the bombardment of Kagoshima by the British fleet—at least that is the story I heard. Anyway, they put on two boats in opposition: the *Komei Maru*, a paddle steamer built at Yokosuka, and the *Capron Maru*, an American tow boat built in America.

Then the underhand work began with the officials on either side, especially at Aomori. Sometimes they would keep the mails and passengers on the beach for six or eight hours and would not let them come on board, waiting to see if the other boat would turn up. Eventually, with other worries, they worried us out of the line.

As there seemed to be no chance of the Japanese putting up the price of the steamer, we were making voyages to Otaru and Muroran and sometimes to Aomori during the later part of the summer, towing junks and anything that turned up.

F

seven

THE MURDER
OF LUDWIG HABER

A TRAGIC EVENT happened in Hakodate during the month of August [1874]. This was nothing less than the murder of Mr. [Ludwig] Haber, the German consul at Hakodate. Mr. Haber was living *pro tem* in the Blakiston, Marr, & Co. house, where I also lived while on shore. Mr. Haber, previous to coming to Japan, had been for some years in Central America, where he contracted malaria fever which seemed to come back on him at times in this country. In appearance he was a small, weak man at his best, and he had been laid up for a week or more with this malaria, confined to the house.

It being August and the college summer holidays, one of the professors, a German friend of Mr. Haber's, came to spend his holidays in Hakodate. We were all dining together between 1 and 2 p.m.—the professor and Mr. Haber and the rest belonging to the house. In conversation during the meal a difference of opinion occurred between Mr. Haber and myself. As the meal was finished, Mr. Haber arose laughing, saying that we would settle the argument at tea time. It was a fine day and he and the professor were going for a walk. Having been confined to the house so long by fever [he was weak], but his friend was a big, burly man and would be able to carry him if he broke down.

They started and walked out the new made road to the tea houses at Yatsugashira, where they rested for some time. Mr.

Haber felt so well that he suggested to the professor that they should take different roads back, Mr. Haber taking the old road, the professor the road they had followed going out, and he said that he would reach the house first. So they separated, according to the professor's account of the parting.

The murderer had come up to Hakodate from Akita prefecture. He was one of those samurai who had sworn to kill foreigners and up to that time in his own country had never come across one he could tackle with a chance of success; at that time few if any foreigners were to be met with in Akita. Hakodate being the nearest open port, he had come seeking his chance. I believe he had been here some weeks, taking stock of all the foreigners he met. He had followed the American consul's son several times, but could not get him by himself in a quiet place. Anyhow, John Hawes, the consul's son, was a tall, active, young lad, for his age, and would not have stood to be cut down.

When the professor and Mr. Haber parted, taking different roads, the man must have been close behind them. [He must have decided to follow Mr. Haber] as Mr. Haber was the smallest and certainly the weakest man and was taking the old road which besides being at first steep, was very lonely. Since the new road had been cut through the ridge, there was only one house on it and a small one at that, with a little patch of garden on the slope of the hill.

The man carried a common Japanese umbrella as well as a concealed sword. When they got opposite the little house, he got up to Mr. Haber and poked him in the back with the umbrella to make him turn around to see if he was a foreigner; then he threw away the umbrella, drew the sword, and cut at him. Mr. Haber, seeing the house and garden, must have run to it, but as far as I could learn there was nobody in it, and if there had been, I question if they would have interfered. Samurai were still feared by the common people. Anyhow, the man followed him, and killed him in the middle of the garden. I found the body there, being the first, with the exception of a solitary policeman, on the scene of the tragedy.

After seeing that his victim was dead, the murderer took the hat and watch off the body, walked into town to the government authorities, and told them what he had done, giving them the hat and watch. The governor immediately sent word to Blakiston, Marr, & Co., in whose house Mr. Haber had been living, also sending word to the British, American and French consuls in Hakodate.

AS MY WORK was mostly night work, I used to sleep afternoons. This afternoon while sleeping, I heard unusual noise outside, got up and went to see what was the matter. Found Captain Blakiston trying to make one of his clerks understand. He wanted him to take four of the boatmen, some rope and a pole, and go as quick as possible to the place where Mr. Haber's body was lying.

To save further trouble, I volunteered to go and, telling the men to get ready, went to put my clothes on, and the five of us went off at the double.

After we had gone some distance, it struck me, as I had only been told that Mr. Haber had been cut down not that he was dead, that I ought to have brought some brandy or other spirits with me. I was about to send a man back, when Captain

Blakiston's last words came back to me—that he would call at the consulate and follow us up. So we started off again.

When we came to the place, I found a policeman standing on the roadway, about forty yards from where the body was lying with its head down hill. I went into the garden patch to have a look and see if there was any life, but one look was enough. The body was fully stretched out, lying a little on its left side. I wanted to turn it over, but the policeman who had followed me up said I must not touch it till the officials came.

After some time the government officials, doctors, and foreign consuls began to turn up. Then the temporary examination of the body began. When finished, I was asked to take charge of the corpse and get it to the government office as quick as possible. My men got a door and *tatami* [mat] from the house on the grounds. When trying to put the body on the mat, we found one leg and one arm hanging by the skin only and three cuts on the head that almost divided it.

When we got to the government office, we found all the officials, consuls and doctors there, sitting in judgment on the murderer, who was kneeling on what they called the *soroban*, with a heavy stone on his knees, to keep him down. This was my first sight of him. He looked like an ordinary Japanese to me, nothing ferocious about him. As the dead body was in the same room in front of him, I wondered what he thought.

As time was getting on, and the men and myself were both tired and hungry, I asked leave to go and get some food as the case seemed to be getting on very slowly. I was told we might go for an hour, but must come back and take the body to the temporary hospital, where the doctors would strip and thoroughly examine the wounds.

It was nearly midnight when we left the hospital. I heard next day the doctors wrought all night at it, examining the wounds and putting it together where it was badly severed. They found 17 wounds on the body, five of which would have been, singly, fatal.

I was sent away next day with a bark and a junk in tow to Kushiro. On my return I was sent with the steamer to Nagasaki to see if the Japanese government would buy her for a steam water tank, General Saigo being at this time down on the east side of Formosa trying to teach the aboriginees of that island. In Nagasaki I heard that the murderer of Mr. Haber was beheaded at Hakodate in the presence of all the foreign consuls to teach the Japanese to behave civilly to strangers and not eat them.

[*eight*]

CARRYING GUNPOWDER
AND SHIP OWNING

WHEN WE GOT to Nagasaki in the later part of September, we found half the foreign settlement in ruins; they had had a severe typhoon that month, which destroyed a lot of property. We also found that General Saigo had finished civilizing or was tired of trying to civilize the Formosans and his troops were returning to Nagasaki, so there was no chance to sell the steamer to them as a water tank. Holme Ringer & Co. were our agents at Nagasaki for the steamer.

The Takashima coal mine had been taken over by the government some two or three years before from the Netherlands Trading Company which, I understand, had taken it over from Glover & Company. They had in their employ a Welshman as mine manager, as well some six miners from Newcastle and Scotland and, as far as I recollect, were turning out some 200 to 250 tons coal daily.

They had employed an old English trinity paddle-steamer, called the *Argus*, owned by a Japanese at Nagasaki, to tow the loaded lighters from the island to Nagasaki and take the empty ones to the island with machinery or stores from Nagasaki, as well as to take the miners and officials to and from the island: one trip per day. This steamer *Argus* had not been able to keep time owing to repairs; being Japanese-owned, they used to patch her up for the day only. When she could not come up to time the officials and others who had to get to and from the island had to take boats and sculls, and they did not like that.

Anyhow, we got a chance, while the *Argus* was laid up for repairs, and we did so well, that they thought they had better charter us for the job. As we wanted them to buy the steamer, I left nothing undone to please them.

After being there some six months, the government thought the mine was not paying and they sold the mine to Mr. Gotō Shōjiro. The firm at No. 1 Yokohama (Jardine Matheson & Co.), I believe, found the money. Then a strange thing happened. The mine, while in government hands, had only turned out some 200 tons of coal per day, but within a month under the new owners the output was 500 to 400 tons per day. This was done by giving the foreign mining engineer a free hand and supplying him with the necessary machinery, so that within less than a year the mine was putting out 700 to 800 tons daily.

In the meantime the *Meishin Maru* was kept on charter by the new mine owners and, as the charter did not give them full control of the steamer, they made an offer to buy the ship and it was accepted. I turned the boat over to them. They still wanted me to stay in command, offering me good pay, but I did not care to stop. It was too easy a job for me in my prime. So they got one of Jardine Matheson's captains from Shanghai to relieve me, and I left for Hakodate.

AFTER being there two weeks, I got tired and wanted to get away afloat again. At this time the late Captain J. Drumond called in at Hakodate in the S/S *Chilli*, under the Japanese flag. She was chartered by the government to go round the ports on the west coast of Nippon and gather all the guns and gunpowder that was left by the different clans after the civil war. As Captain Drumond had not been round the west coast ports, he asked me to go with him. It would cost me nothing and as he was to call at Sado Island, I took the chance to call and see James Scott the engineer at the Sado Mines.

The first port we called at was Niigata in the latter part of July [1875]. We found the heavy guns that were to be taken away were some six feet under water; the river being in flood and having risen some 12 feet. In fact, with the exception of one or two places, the whole town was under water to the depth of two or three feet.

Knowing the German consul at Niigata, I went to see him and stayed two days with him. Made inquiries about what time the river was likely to get back to normal but all I could learn was that it might be ten or twenty days before they could begin to ship the guns. I said I would not stop all that time and asked him to get his servant to engage a ricksha for me to take me to a village some twelve miles from Niigata, where I could get a horse to carry me to Teradomari (this was the place from where the mails were carried across by boat to Sado Island) as I had some official letters for the officials there. He pooh-poohed the matter; said I had no passport and Teradomari was outside the treaty limits; they would stop me and bring me back. I told him I was going anyhow.

Next morning got a ricksha and started. When leaving, the consul said he would wait dinner for me, I said:

'No fear, I'll get through.'

We started about 7 a.m.

I must say the ricksha man was a brick. As we left the higher part of the town, getting on the outskirts, we got into a part of the country that was flooded. Water at first about two inches, but later it began to get deeper; still later it got to eight inches or more. Still the man toiled on. I stopped him and asked if there was much more of this to go through. He said about one or two *ri* [Japanese miles], so I told him to hold on, I would get out and walk. Taking my boots, stockings, and trousers off and leaving them in the ricksha, I got out and walked. The road seemed good under foot, but that 5 miles seemed the longest I ever walked. At last we got to the village, where we were to stop, and had lunch. The next part of the way was mostly uphill.

I chartered a horse, paid and let the rickshaman go. The new pilot I got started downhill and we got into a flooded road with over one foot of water. I said that would not do as the horses were stumbling in holes. Went back to the inn again and asked if there was no other road. They said there was one along the foot of the hill, but the way was longer. I said, never mind; we took the hill road and arrived at Teradomari about 6 p.m. tired and dirty.

Now came the question about a passport—I could understand that much from the landlord's talk. They had brought me water to wash my hands and feet; in fact, they were very kind. As I have said, I had some letters for the officials at Sado Island. Taking my coat off to wash myself, I purposely dropped the letters and as they had the large Kobusho red stamp on them, they said among themselves, he is all right, and I heard no more about a passport.

It had been bad weather for some days and no mails had

gone across to the island for three days, but they were in hopes of being able to cross the next morning. After having a bath, I went to sleep and knew nothing till 4 o'clock next morning.

The inn was full of people, all hands were turned out to wash and get breakfast, as the boats were to leave at once. When I was ready, they took me down and put me in the mail boat, the only passenger. All the others were in other boats; some six altogether left that morning. We had a fine passage of a little over two and half hours across.

When I landed on the island, I was asked if I wanted a horse or a *kago* [palanquin] to take me to Aikawa. Said no, would walk; thought I knew as much about the island as the people belonging to it. Looking at the island from the sea, Sado Island looks like two parallel ridges running in N.E. and S.W. direction, joined in the middle of their length by the lowland at Ebisu village, and my idea was that I only had to climb up to the top and slide down the other side to Futami bay.

It must have been about 8 o'clock when I started, and a roasting hot day. It was lucky the road was good and well marked, but the way was long to the top and I would rest for a little under the trees. It took me over five hours to get across the ridge to the bay on the other side. When I came to the village at the bay, I found all hands were having a sleep in the heat of the day. Could get nothing to eat, but eventually managed to get two fishermen to put me across the bay to Futami village.

From Futami it was a good three miles to Scott's house at Aikawa. When I got there my clothes were sticking to my body and quite hard with sweat. Although I had eaten nothing all day I was too tired to eat at Scott's house; had a bath and went to bed.

It was ten days later that the *Chilli* turned up at Futami and a week later before she left again for Nanao in Noto Peninsula, where we took in a lot of gunpowder in very bad condition; boxes broken and powder leaking. From Nanao we went to Sakata; took in powder again. It was in even worse condition than before. It simply frightened one to see how the coolies handled the dangerous stuff.

From Sakata the *Chilli* was to go to Aomori for more guns and powder, then finish up by going to Hakodate for coal before taking her cargo to Shinagawa. In the Tsugaru Straits the engineer told Captain Drumond he had only one day's coal left and not knowing what might happen, it would be better to go to Hakodate and get coal first. This we did, and I was never more pleased to get out of a ship than the *Chilli*, half full of gunpowder. However, they got to Shinagawa all right, but there were not many of the foreigners on board till the cargo was all out and the holds cleaned out

HAVING nothing to do, got tired of loafing around. Went in for ship owning [1876]. Some two years previous, the firm of Thompson & Bewick, shipbuilders & compradores, had built a vessel of 120 [tons] register, brigantine-rigged. They had run her on their own account, but lost money on her, not being able to get or pay a decent master for her. They were heavily in debt all around. Between the creditors and debtors they persuaded me to buy her, as I was able to go master of her myself. This was one of the greatest mistakes I ever made.

As a shipmaster I was noted for taking big risks, i.e. going to places that were unsafe even with other peoples property, but was always lucky until I came to handle my own property; then my luck left me with this and two other vessels I owned and sailed.

The first one I sailed two years and made some money, then while lying off the northwestern coast of Hokkaido, loading salmon, she blew on shore, with [in spite of] four anchors down, on a sandy beach. Tried to get her off, but with winter coming on had to leave her and came on to Hakodate. She was not insured.

Not caring to risk the expense of launching her, though the hull and masts were not damaged, sold her to a Japanese (1877). When I settled up accounts, just came out even: no gain no loss.

Then, as if I not had enough, through interested advice I had another schooner built—this time to go sea-otter hunting. By the time she was finished and ready for sea, half the season was gone; but we managed to get seventy otters. The life of otter hunters—keeping ship to clean skins—did not suit me. When the season was finished we came back to Hakodate and I sold ship and catch. This deal did not turn out right.

[nine]

SALVAGING A
RUSSIAN DISPATCH BOAT

DURING the time that I was in Hakodate, a Russian dispatch vessel was driven on shore on the west coast. She was bound from Nikolaevsk. That year the Russian government was making their naval headquarters at Vladivostok and the dispatch vessel was carrying naval stores from the old station on the Amur to the new one at Vladivostok.

Her name was the *Rupak*. She was built at St. Petersburg of heavy iron plates, had two masts square-rigged, the regular naval horizontal engines and two boilers.

In a hurry to get away before the river froze up, the Russians had left without sufficient coal, trusting to their sails to help them. They trusted a rotten stick.

It was late autumn and the strong west and N.W. winds blew them across the Japan Sea to the coast of Yesso. They had passed Otaru, where they might have run to with a fair wind and got coal, but that did not strike them; they were trying to make for Hakodate. As it was blowing hard, they got embayed between two high-bluff headlands. In the centre of the bay, between two rivers, was a fine sandy beach about two miles in length. After letting go their anchors with all their chain, they stranded almost in the center of this beach.

All hands got on shore and they saved all their clothes and ship's gear, and another Russian transport came and took away all the crew but one lieutenant and twelve seamen and an

G

engineer and eight firemen who remained to keep watch. These men got a house built on shore. Lining it with sails outside and inside to keep out the cold, they had cooking and other stoves. As they had to cut down wood to build their house, there was no want of firewood.

The irony of the thing was that the Japanese government sent up a posse of police to see that the Russians did not cut the wood at their own door, and made them buy all the firewood they wanted for use.

There were no houses nor people living on this two mile stretch of sandy beach between the two rivers. To get to the Japanese villages either of the rivers had to be crossed, and the Russians had no boats. They had to cross the rivers by the ferry boats. Said ferry boats, with boatmen's houses, were on the far side of the river from the Russians, so one policeman at each river could keep stock of any of the Russians that wanted to go to the villages to buy anything or of any Japanese taking anything to sell.

As this was in pre-extraterritorial days, every foreigner had to get passports to travel outside treaty limits. None of the Russians were allowed to cross either of the rivers without permission; everything they wanted had to be got through the authorities.

As the *Rupak* lay exposed to the winter gales and heavy seas, everything above her decks was swept away—masts, bulwarks, funnel, and hatches—and she soon filled up with sand and water. The lieutenant reported this, and the Russian government decided to sell her by auction in the Russian consulate at Yokohama.

AS I WAS IDLE, I was asked to go in and bid for her. I telegraphed down to Mr. Frank Spooner of Carroll & Co. at Yokohama to bid as high as 1,000 dollars for the *Rupak* on my account and I left the next day by steamer for Yokohama to look for a job as well as to see the outcome of the sale. Instead of landing at Yokohama, the steamer went to Shinagawa. It being Saturday afternoon I went to Tokyo, where I spent Sunday and the half of Monday getting to Yokohama. After office hours, however, I went to Carroll & Co. and saw Mr. Spooner. He told me the wreck was knocked down to him and that he had gone 50 dollars over the amount I had telegraphed to him, and that if I was not pleased he would take her himself. I said, no, that 50 dollars either way made no difference.

The next thing was to get the Japanese government's permission to work at the wreck and both Mr. Spooner and myself thought that since she was a Russian gunboat, the Russian minister was the man to get government permission to work at the wreck. So Mr. Spooner had an interview with the Russian consul who had sold the wreck, telling him that I was the owner of the *Rupak*, and asking him to get the permit to work through his minister. He said he would write to his minister and ask him.

The Russian minister, seeing by the consul's letter to him that the new owner of the *Rupak* was a British subject, referred the matter to Sir H. Parkes, the British minister, who knowing me personally, wondered why I had applied to the Russian minister to help me, and wrote to Mr. Robertson, British consul at Yokohama, asking if I had applied to him or if he knew where I lived. Consul Robertson, knowing that Carroll & Co. were the agents, wrote me a letter care of them, asking me to call and see him. When we met, his first words were:

'When did you become a Russian subject?' Why had I applied to the Russian minister for help?, he [wanted to know] and he told me that Sir Harry, the Minister, was much surprised that I should call on the Russian minister for help, and had asked the consul, in his letter, if I had asked him for help.

The outcome of it was that I had the necessary permission within twenty-four hours. Besides, Sir Harry Parkes wrote to the consul at Hakodate to give me all assistance in his power with the local authorities at Hakodate.

I could do nothing at the *Rupak* while the winter winds were blowing; did not attempt to go near her till the end of March. In fact, it was not possible to go earlier; there was only one way to get there, and that was by walking. There were at that time no small steamers running along the coast in winter, and I had to wait till the coolies went herring fishing to make a road through the snow, crossing the mountains. The first twelve miles, to the foot of the hills were done on horseback; but from there it was four and half days 'shanks mare'.

The walking was done in Japanese *waraji* [straw sandals]; boots of any kind were no good. I tried them the first day climbing a hill, covered with deep snow. While wearing boots, I had to get two men ahead to tow me up. When I discarded the boots and got *waraji* I could keep time with the others. When we got through the mountains to the west coast, the only road was the sea beach, and every few miles we had to cross little streams which were running full of water since the snow was melting. As there was no other way to get across, we simply had to take them in our stride. Here is where the *waraji*, came in handy. Boots would have had to be taken off and put on again. Some of the streams were as much as three feet deep, so that tucking trowsers up was no good. I never did so, but just walked across, as I have said, in my stride. When we got to the *yado* [lodgings] where we stopt for the night, all wet clothes were taken off and hung up above the large wood fire in the general room and were always dry, though hard, in the morning. With a little rubbing to soften them and with new *waraji* we were all fit for another day's travel.

I may say here that hotels, such as they were in Hokkaido in those days [1878] were not expensive as now. My passport called for the best *yado* wherever I stopt. Before I left Hakodate, my servant was given a book by the authorities and was told to take it to the *nanushi* [elder] in every village we stopt at. The latter would provide a house for us and put down the amount charged at each place we stopt. He put his stamp to it as being correct. This book was brought back to Hakodate and examined by the authorities; woe betide any one that overcharged us.

I can only say that though my boy and myself almost always had a room to ourselves, the expense was never more than the eqivalent of 60 sen in present-day [*ca.* 1899] money. For both of us supper, a bed, breakfast, and *obento* [box lunch] for the midday meal, a mighty difference from present-day charges.

The village of Settanai, where we took up our quarters till the Russian crew vacated the house they had built at the wreck, was three miles past the wreck, but was the nearest and largest village in the bay. We took up our quarters in the same house as the superintendent of police, who was in charge of the men that were looking after the Russian crew. I had stayed an hour with the Russian officers on my way, but had to leave to get to the village before dark to settle about a house to live in.

Next day after breakfast went to the wreck and spent the day with the officers at the house. I found the house they had built to winter in made thoroughly wind and water tight with canvas and flags; besides, in the crew's end, they had the cooking range from the ship, and a stove from the officer's mess in their end. As they could not get in or out the house for growing timber, there was no lack of firewood handy, though the Japanese made them pay for all they used.

I stayed about a week at the village, paying a visit daily to the Russians at the wreck. The month of February being, you might say, mid-winter, the regular winter winds and snow blowing, I was unable to get an idea of what the wreck was like and went back to Hakodate. There I heard from the Russian consul that:

'In April, when the winter winds are finished, the crew at the wreck will be taken off by a transport.'

I paid another visit to Settanai and the wreck in the latter part of March. Stayed a few days—two or three of which were fine—and was able to get on board and get some idea of the job I had to tackle.

I found she was embedded in the sand and as full of sand as an egg of meat. This probably kept the hull from being damaged during the winter gales. There were five feet of water above her stem, and her stern was as much above water, when the sea was calm. But a clean sweep had been made of every thing above the level of the deck with the exception of the hatch coaming; even the stoke hole grating had been swept away.

On my return to Hakodate, I asked Mr. Thompson, the shipbuilder who had had some experience the year before at Iwanai with a Japanese schooner, loaded with manure, on a sandy beach like the *Rupak*.

Nothing was to be got at Settanai village; everything had to be got at Hakodate. The gear bought for the work was not expensive but bulky—100 empty saké tubs and 1000 empty rice bags. There was plenty of all kinds of rope belonging to the wreck. Having bought the above and settled to get it carried to Settanai, I engaged a carpenter, a sawyer, two sailors and a cook—five men in all—and left for Settanai overland.

I had left my boy behind on my previous trip, to take over the house and gear from the Russians should they be taken away while I was at Hakodate.

As it happened, the transport arrived while I was away and took the Russian crew or part of them. The transport had to anchor a mile off the beach; sent a large cutter to take off the men and their belongings. A light breeze was blowing in from the sea, which gradually freshened, causing a lipper [a sea which washes over the bow] on the water. One boat got away all right and came back for the remainder, dropt its anchor to keep the boat head on to wind and sea, which with the freshening wind [was] rising to wavelets.

When the last of the men were got in the boat, there was some trouble getting the anchor up. They were so anxious to get away, they lost their heads, and instead of cutting or slipping the anchor rope, they crowded as many men on the bow of the boat as could stand, all pulling at the anchor rope.

In consequence the boat went down by the head, the water lippered on board, and the boat filled and went from under them, leaving them all in the water.

Luckily my boy and a few other Japanese were on the beach seeing them off, as were the policemen who had been looking after the Russian crew. By rushing into the sea they managed to get some dozen men on shore, but eleven men were drowned. My boy was conspicuous in this; he dragged five men on shore safe, and the Russian government a year later presented him with a gold medal.

The transport sent another boat in charge of a proper officer and took away the sunken cutter and the men that were saved, and cleared out for Vladivostok. I heard all this story from the boy when I reached the wreck from Hakodate.

Before leaving for the wreck I had made arrangements to get my stores and gear sent up by junk about the beginning of May, as well as forty coolies when I was ready for them to begin work.

With the six men I had (carpenter, sawyer, and sailors), we started in to plug and fill up all the holes. There were some twenty light ports on each side; and besides other holes, some dozen hatches, companions, and sky lights to cofferdam or otherwise make water tight. Made what the Japanese call *mukko* for lifting the sand out of the wreck, and got ropes ready to sling the saké tubs for bailing out the water.

There was no want of material—the running rigging of the wreck for rope and on the beach any quantity of timber that had been blown across the Japan Sea during the winter gales from the coast of Manchuria opposite. So all the carpenter had to do was go along the beach, pick out the log he wanted, get all hands to put it up for the sawyer to cut, chalk out the thickness of the planks he wanted, then set the sawyer to work. All of us wrought with a will, so that by the end of May we had got everything made water tight, the hatches coffer-damed.

I sent a man to Hakodate to tell them to send the coolies as soon as possible, as the east summer winds were coming on which gave us smooth water. The coolies landed at Esashi from a vessel and walked from there to the wreck in a day and half. Our chow and stores had been landed a few days earlier at Settanai, so when the coolies came we had everything ready for a start. We gave the coolies a day to get settled down in their quarters and look about them.

The next day being fine, we made a start to bail the water out of the captain's and officer's quarters aft, that being the only part of the vessel above water. After bailing for two hours we found the water in her did not amount to much, for in that two hours we had all the water out of the two aft compartments. Then we found we had a ship full of hard banked wet sand to deal with.

Next day started to get the water out of the engine room, stoke hole, and small hold which, I was informed, was full of naval stores. We got all the water out and came down to the sand. In the hold we came on a lot of Muntz-metal sheets, which was half worn (had been stripped of some vessel's bottom) and some large rough wooden casks full of tallow, and some coils of running rigging.

As it had started to blow from seaward, made everything secure and watertight. Sent to the village to get some tools to work the wet sand.

For two days the sea was breaking over the vessel, but there was plenty of work making *mukko* ready to get the sand out. After two days' rest, everyone started with a will to tackle the sand; every one seemed to have made up their minds that the ship was to be lifted and taken to Hakodate. But it was a hard slow job. The men's hands got sore pulling on the ropes, wet with salt water and covered with sand. Still, as the ship seemed to be tight and every lift was making the sand less, this kept encouraging them and they kept at it.

But when we had got all the sand cleared out of the engine room and stoke hole, the sea cock used by the firemen for cooling their ashes, which they had broken after the vessel began to fill, thinking the water would run out, and which had been stopt with the hard sand, got a knock from the iron with which they were cleaning the sand out. The water started to rush in and all hands had to get on deck.

Now the trouble began how to stop the leak. We must get at it outside. We dug away the sand for about ten feet along the ship's side. A man got down and found the intake, but there was an iron grating almost flush with the outside, so it could not be plugged. The next thing was to cofferdam abreast the intake. This we did by driving down posts, then, filling rice bags with sand, we dumped them down between the posts and the ship, trusting one would catch the intake. Then we started [again] to bail out the water, which was soon done. Having got everything to fix the pipe, stopt the leak for good. Another small [leak] in the large cofferdam over one of the hatches during a gale was the only other trouble we had barring occasional strong winds from off sea.

Eventually we got everything out of her. She rose out of the sand herself. The next thing was to get her afloat. We laid out chains and anchors, and as she had only one capstan (and that from being under water and sand for six months was not of much use), we made Japanese, wooden capstans and started to haul off the shore. She came slowly at first, but keeping the pull on her all the time, in less than half a day we had her afloat and riding at anchor half a mile off shore.

I started a man off to Hakodate with a letter to tell them the ship was afloat and engage some steamer to tow us to Hakodate. Next day we started to get the gear and stores we had found, on board of her again and, as everyone wanted to get back to Hakodate, this was done in two and half days. Then there was nothing to do but wait for the steamer coming for us a couple days later.

While we were looking for help from Hakodate, the government steamer *Hakodate Maru* came to tow us; she came from Otaru having been advised from Hakodate. She had two tow ropes ready to pass the ends on board, and when we got them fast and our anchor hove up, we started for Hakodate, where we safely arrived twenty hours after leaving Settanai.

The folks in Hakodate were on the lookout for us; had a man on the hill. On opening up the harbour, we saw all the foreign houses had their flags hoisted to welcome us. The consul telegraphed to Sir Harry Parkes, and he telegraphed back congratulations on our success in lifting and bringing the Russian gunboat to Hakodate.

[ten]

SHIPWRECKED

AFTER lifting and bringing the Russian gun boat *Rupak* to Hakodate, I bought from Messers. Thompson & Bewick a vessel they were building of some 300 tons deadweight [October, 1878]. After fitting her out, got a charter to go to one of the outlying islands (Taraku) and load all the seaweed collected there and bring back the coolies to Hakodate. It being late in the year we had to hurry up, there being no safe anchorage.

After loading most of the seaweed it came on to blow from eastward; had with a great deal of trouble and risk to shift and get better shelter.

After two days we got back again, got balance of cargo and coolies on board, and with the last of daylight got underway and left for Nemuro. Wind blowing fresh from westward. After clearing the outlying rocks, steered north between the islands, intending to work down between the islands and Kunashiri to Nemuro, as on that course my chart showed no hidden dangers. There being a fresh working breeze, I lay down on the cabin floor on a mattress, cabin door open, clothes on, ready to jump out.

I had not got to sleep, though dead tired, when the cry went out:

'Breakers ahead!' I jumped out, saw the white break.

'Put helm up. Lower down the peak of the mainsail!' I called out. Ship paid off quickly, but her starboard bilge struck a ridge, and as she was going six to eight knots, she rushed over the ridge yet tore the bilge away. All hands and the coolies, some forty in number, rushed on deck. Ship brought to, pumps sounded and started, but we found the damage was too great; no chance of keeping afloat till daylight.

Having so many people on board, some sixty all told, and only one boat, the next thing to do was to run for Shakotan and see if we could pick out a soft place or creek [to beach] to save what we could.

Before we got close to the island so much water leaked in that she was getting unmanageable. Seeing a break between the hills, put her for the break as the water seemed smooth, not broken. But the vessel had sunk so much that she struck a ledge and brought up suddenly; the water in her went to one side and she turned over on that side with the masts in the water.

Our boat had washed away and there was no sign of any houses or people on shore. All of the coolies and crew were hanging to the rigging or the ship's side that was out of the water.

After daylight some good swimmers among the men managed to swim on shore by resting on the rocks on the way. First one man managed to get safe ashore, then others followed; four or five men all together. Then they set out to look for help. After a time they picked up a house and some shacks, in which there were some three men that were left behind to look after the place in the winter. All coolies and produce having gone to Nemuro some ten days before, their boats were all hauled on shore and covered up for the winter.

However, they managed to launch a large *mo chip*, a boat that would carry about ten or twelve people. Keeping inshore, inside the outer rocks, they managed to get opposite the ship, where they found quite a swell and fresh breeze blowing on shore. By making a struggle they managed to get alongside. I told them not to take too many in the first boat. As all were anxious to get ashore, I made them push off. Luckily as the day made, the wind went down a little, and, as the men got on shore and rested a bit, there was a fresh crew to pull the boat off again, so the work went on quicker. After four or five trips all [were ashore] with the exception of my servant and two men who were left on board.

The men and myself were standing on the side of the cabin. As the crowd had gone, things were quiet and we heard knocking inside the cabin, as if there was someone alive inside. So we rapped back and got an answer. As there was no means of getting at the man but by making a hole in the ship's side and as everything on board had gone or was underwater, we would have to get tools from shore, and as the man was quite safe unless the ship broke up, I agreed to go on shore in the last boat as I thought I would be able to hurry matters. But I did not count on the darkness; was unable to get any of the crew or coolies to start back to the ship that night.

As I could not sleep, thinking of the man still on board, I got up early, got a meal cooked. We had collected axes and saws and appointed a dozen volunteers to go off with me. Had a boat launched and started for the wreck. The weather had quieted down and all were anxious to get on board and get the poor fellow out of his prison. When we got him out, we found he had been quite dry and warm, but had felt his loneliness, knowing all the others had left the wreck and the uncertainty of his position.

As it was so late in the year and there was no chance of another vessel coming to take us off the island till next spring and there was no food on the island for so many extra men, the thing was how to get back to Nemuro.

It was arranged that we were to get three large fishing boats and pull back from island to island, a hard job to face. We got as much rice as could be spared and a rice boiler with plenty of water. The coolies knew where the winter watchmen were to be found on the different islands, trusting that if short of food we might get some help. We started in two boats, leaving six men of the crew to salve or pick up anything that might come on shore—sails or spare cargo.

As far as I can recollect, we were some eight days in the boats before we got to Suisho Island, the nearest to Cape Noshappu [the MS. gives Noshapt]. Here we found a junk at anchor. The captain proving a good Samaritan, took us all on board, gave us hot food and let us rest all day—the really first sleep we had since starting from Shakotan Island.

I might mention that the Captain told us the thermometer was down to zero the day before we got to the junk. As all our clothes had been lost except for what we had on, the cold we had put up with in the seven nights we spent in the open boats with no other covering than the boat's sail was something to talk about; besides, the food was simply rice balls; no kitchen. (As I have often said since, a man does not know what he can stand till put to it.)

After the rest and a hot meal we started early to cross the Noshappu Strait to the main island. When we arrived at Nemuro, there was one of the small Mitsubishi steamers, *Seiryo Maru*, in the harbour, the Captain an old friend; and

I got the boatman to put me alongside. Though late at night and all had been asleep, they were so surprised when they found who it was and what had happened to me and my ship, they could not believe it at first. When they realized that we had come from Shakotan [the MS. states Sakatan] in open boats with the cold weather they had for the last ten days, they could hardly believe it.

Then they started to get a hot bath ready and a change of clothes, all the officers and engineers almost fighting as to who could do the best for me. The cook was turned out and hot food got ready, hot whisky and brandy, all pressing that his was better than the other fellow's: the same about the clothes I was to put on. Later they saw that I was tired; they thought that a bed was what I wanted most after what I had gone through the last ten days.

In the morning when I got on shore and reported to the authorities, being well known to all the reputable people in Nemuro as the pioneer foreigner, in a foreign-built vessel, to enter Nemuro harbour and to come through the Noshappu Straits, the people could not show enough sympathy for me when they found out I had lost my all and was penniless.

However, as I was still in my prime, it was no use to cry over it. The thing was to get back to Hakodate and settle with crew and creditors.

H

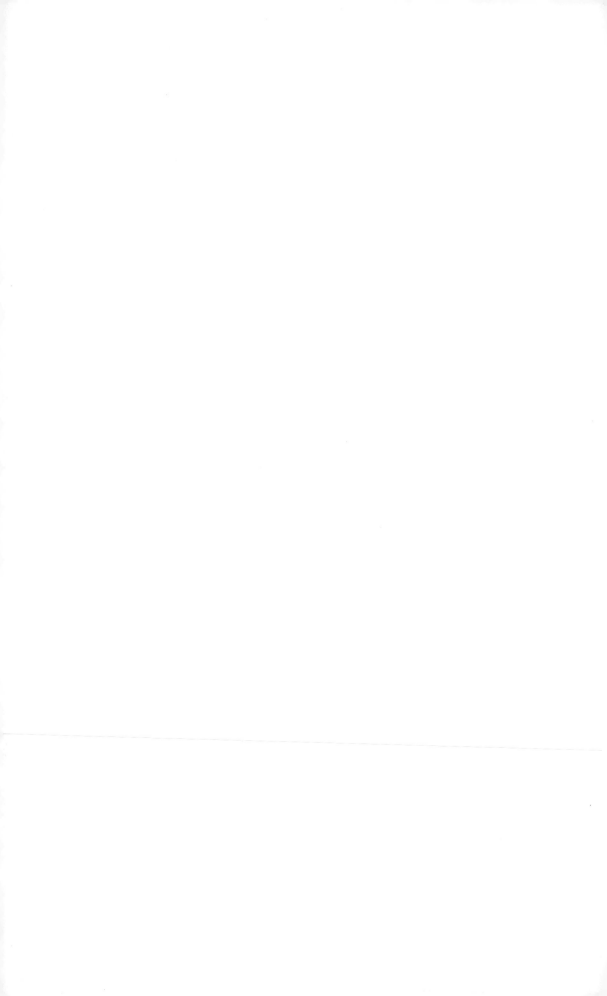

eleven

A NAPOLEONIC CAPTAIN

MY CREW and myself got passage in the *Seiryo Maru*. As I had no money—only ¥1,800 left by me in the consul's hands, [from] the sale of the Russian gunboat *Rupak*—when my creditors were all called [my debts] amounted to ¥6,500. So I was advised by a friend of mine to become a bankrupt and go through the court. The knowledge of bankruptcy courts of the consul in Hakodate at that time was nil and the time it took him to refer to books for information was so long I got tired and asked him to let me go to Yokohama to look for work; but no, he kept me hanging on.

In the meantime I had to live, and he had to allow me out of the money he had in hand to keep me, thus reducing the amount for my creditors. A friend of mine at the gold mines in Sado sent me ¥200 to be paid at Yokohama by his agents there. As my friend, Mr. J. A. Wilson of Howell & Co., undertook to look after my bankrupt affairs here and was later appointed trustee of my estate, I left for Yokohama. . . .

The Mitsubishi Company had taken over the Pacific Mail coasting-steamers, old wooden paddle steamers; as well some old English steamers, some three of which they had gutted of all machinery and rigged out with masts and sails as training ships for Japanese boys. There was likely to be a chance of work for me, as I held both English and Japanese master's certificates. But though it was work I wanted, I was anxious to take the first and any job I could get, being a little ashamed to show myself after my come down. In all the years I had been in and about Japan, this was the first time I had had to look for work, and I was a little diffident.

After two or three days I met Captain Burgess, the marine superintendent of the Mitsubishi Company. He said he wondered why I had not looked him up, as he heard I had come down looking for work. He said there were [few] masters wanted, but come along to his office. I told him it was a question of getting work—even mate or 2nd mate—as long as I was earning my living, as I was bankrupt and did not want to get more in debt.

While in the office, Captain Wynn of one of the Shanghai mail steamers came in to see the superintendent. His 2nd mate had left or was sick and the mail steamer had to leave. Wondering to see me at the office and hearing I was asking for work of any kind, he said to the superintendent I might go a trip or two with him and I would be able to look about at the different ports she called at till something better turned up. I said I would go.

The superintendent was much pleased, saying he would not forget me. Captain Wynn and I were old friends and I was pleased to start again, climbing with an old friend to help me. Both the superintendent and Captain Wynn knew there was none knew the coast of Japan and North China from experience better than I did; who could get through the Inland Sea or into any of the ports without pilots.

THE *Oregonian* was one of the oldest of the wooden paddle steamers, taken over from the Pacific Mail. She was the first ship I was afraid being on board of at sea. Having no bridge, the officer's watch was kept on the fore deck, and as there was nothing but the wheel house on the upper deck, you could see clear to the stern. Between Nagasaki and Shanghai, both ways, we sometimes had headwinds and sea and looking along the deck when the stern lifted or fell with the sea, the deck used to lift or fall as if she would break in the middle.

Another thing, the 3rd class passengers on the lower deck had to be carefully watched; often a hundred or more, mostly of the labouring class; no smoking allowed and only the deck lanterns. Besides watchmen, the quartermaster off turn at the wheel had to go down and look around, come up and report to the officer on watch every half hour. These old wooden paddle steamers, all the time I was in them, looked to me like match boxes; if fire once started, nothing could stop it although the fire hoses were stretched regularly every night. I never felt safe all the time I was on board them.

The *Oregonian* was laid up for machinery repairs. I was put on reserve on board the reserve ship, one of the old paddle steamers, for some days. Then I got orders to join one of the shire boats they had bought, as mate. A Captain Frahm, a Dane, was in command of her.

Frahm was one of that kind of men mates could not get along with. He used to stand on the bridge with his arms crossed à la Napoleon and shout his orders from there, especially if close to shipping in port, as much as to say 'look at me.' Mates would not stop with him, so I was sent with him. I made two or three voyages with him. He pretended that he knew all about the Japan coast although in his heart he knew different.

ONE NIGHT, going through the Inland Sea, intending to go through the northern passage—my watch on deck—the captain was forward, conning the ship as he thought. When we got to the top of the passage and he still kept on into Mihara Bay instead of turning at right angles, I shouted:

'We will be ashore directly, we have passed the passage!' He started as if he had been asleep.

'Stop her! Go astern full speed! and stand by to anchor.'

'No need of that,' I said. 'It's a fine clear night and there is the passage open on the port quarter. Swing her stern round on port helm till she points for the passage, then go ahead all, right down the passage.'

The story got about at Yokohama, though not from me; it was about in Yokohama before we got back.

We had to get on board that voyage at Kobe, alongside the pier, two locomotive engines and other railway gear bound to Tsuruga for the railway they were making round Lake Biwa to Tsuruga. Now, the rail track on the pier was at least eight feet from the ship's side and as the boilers weighed at least ten tons and the only gear we had on board for lifting weights were booms equal to three or four tons and our worthy captain was walking the opposite side of the pier with the captain of another steamer that was lying there, I went across to him and asked him who was to put them on board. He said we were.

'Well, how are coolies coming to lift them on board? We have no gear to lift them boilers on board.'

'Oh,' he said, 'that no trouble.'

'All right,' I said, 'you had better boss the job yourself.' That he daren't tackle, so he said:

'Tell me what gear you want and I'll tell the agent to get it.'

'Besides gear,' I told him, 'before I start, the railway people will have to take the wheels off the engine and all the other gear that can be taken off, lift and slide the boiler some four or five feet closer to the ship's side.'

I told him what blocks and ropes I wanted.

Well, next day ropes, blocks and gear came along. Luckily the second mate was a sailing ship man, so we settled over-night between us just what we would have to rig up.

The steamer was square rigged; on the foremast she carried a fore and topsail yard. This helped us, as we were able to rig a derrick at the side of the ship, by taking the lift from the wharf. We could not have lifted the boiler without this help as the distance was too great between lift and ship for the only spar we could get for the middle derrick. The second mate got the boiler slung, but it was just a little off the centre weight when we started to lift it. Of course, the second mate was not to blame for this, using his own judgment; there ought to have been some one from the railway department there to see the boiler slung. Anyhow, the critics on the pier, among whom was the captain of the vessel, after seeing what happened cried:

'Old Will can't do it.'

Among the critics was the chief engineer of the steamer lying opposite. After he heard them saying we could not lift it, he told them to hold on a minute. As I have said, we had two square yards on the foremast. Seeing that a watch tackle could do all that was needed, we lashed the topsail yard to the lower mast head and the halyards which were on that side of the ship. We put a strop round the boiler, hooked the halyards on, and with two man pulling, the boiler was level. Now the trouble came. There were only two steam winches and their power was not equal to the lift, so we had to lead the main lifting gear to the steam windlass. After firing up on the donkey boiler all it would stand, we got the boiler and some trucks on board. Started for Tsuruga.

Here again we had trouble.

He was one of those men who always wanted his anchor buoyed. Proper thing to do except for his idea of bringing his ship to anchor. At Tsuruga we had the whole harbour—some square miles of it—to ourselves. He would go astern, stop the ship dead with a turn ahead; this brought the bouy rope in a coil right under the anchor. The several times he had done this before [he] let go the anchor. Of course, it fouled the bouy rope; anchor gone, the bouy was not visible. Then the anchor had to be hove up and the bouy cleared, then ahead and astern, and the bouy rope coil under the anchor again let go. I called out to him that the bouy was still foul of the anchor.

'Give a turn of the engine either way to clear the rope, do not let go the anchor.'

I got angry and went aft to the bridge. He was standing up there with his arms crossed and a supercillious smile on his face, as much as to say, 'look at me I am the only man in this ship.' I asked what he meant. He asked did I think this was a small ship like what I had been used to handle? I told him to go forward and I would go on the bridge and give him a lesson in handling a ship. However, we got the anchor down at last. Our locomotives out; knowing how we took them in, we had all the gear on board for doing so. Back to Yokohama.

A Napoleonic captain

OUR NEXT voyage was to Fusan, then to Gensan. Some six government officials came on board as passangers. We had previously taken on board house building material and other stores. Among the officials was the first consul or minister to Gensan, Korea. We called at Fusan first. Got a pilot for Gensan, as our charts at that time (1880) were not very plain. I was much surprised at the size and appearance of the harbour. We quickly got rid of our passangers and stores.

Among the officials there was a doctor whom I had met in Saghalien some ten years before; he was in charge of the Japanese colony there when I was carrying emigrants from Hakodate to that place. He was surprised to see me as mate in that steamer. I did not tell all that had happened since seeing him last, but he told the other officials about our first meeting and they were pleased to ask all about what I could tell them of Japan. At the table they would keep talking to or at me. The captain did not like that the officials should take so much notice of me.

BACK IN JAPAN I made one or two more voyages in the steamer. The captain had asked me why I did not ask for a change; he did not like me. I told him one time to ask for a change himself, as I could stand it as long as he could, but he must have applied to the head office to change me. Coming to Yokohama after a voyage, the superintendent came on board and said to me:

'Will, are you not tired of this ship yet?' Said he was going to take the second engineer and me both out. I must say here that the second engineer and myself had for some time had our meals in our own rooms; we refused to go to the saloon table to eat our meals, so things had been getting pretty hot. The chief and 3rd engineers and the 2nd mate only went to eat in the saloon occasionally, and the captain did not like it. So he must have asked the head office to change us.

The 2nd engineer was taken on shore and appointed assistant superintendent engineer; I was put on reserve and for the rest of the four years I was in the company I was only some six or eight months in actual work on good pay. I was only appointed when some special work was wanted, such as at a wreck of one of the sailing ships, or if a sick captain wanted to be relieved for a voyage I was sent to relieve him.

ONE TIME a mate was wanted for one of the sailing ships. There were some twenty officers in the reserve ship. Looking them all over, the captain and superintendent said there was only one man in the crowd who could be called fit to go mate of a sailing ship, and they thought I would refuse. But I jumped at the job. I was tired of loafing about Yokohama, doing nothing but drinking.

This was one of my most pleasant jobs while in the company. Unfortunately I only made the one voyage. I was wanted on reserve for anything that might turn up that wanted a man with knowledge of navigation anywhere round Japan. Then came the old round again, loafing and drinking.

MY NEXT TRIP, I think, was taking a towboat to Oginohama. I was supposed to anchor every night, i.e. only run in daylight.

I refused, saying of anchorages between Yokohama and Ogi-nohama I knew of none after leaving Tokyo Bay. This was sent to the head office. Answer sent back:

'Let Will go as he likes as long as the steamer gets to Ogi-nohama.'

So we left. Got there in some 28 hours, long before we were expected. As I had to wait some three days before the boat I was to take back to Yokohama would be back, and as Ogi-nohama was rather a dull place—only Japanese food to be got, there being no company steamers in port I could live on board of—I asked the agent if I could not cross the bay to Sendai. He said, all right.

[*twelve*]

TO SENDAI
WITHOUT PASSPORT

THE BOAT I had brought up was to leave early in the morning to cross the bay. I got away in her and landed on the Sendai side all right; landed and walked up to the town. Got there about 6 p.m. as far as I can recollect. Had a look at the place.

As I walked round, came to a big three-storied house which turned out to be a first class hotel. I got in and asked them to give me a room for the night as I was going back to Oginohama in the morning by ricksha. Seeing I was a foreigner, there was some trouble; but later they gave me a room and food. I signed their book for the police. As I was tired, got them to make up a bed and turned in about 9 o'clock. Just as I had got asleep, in comes a servant and a policeman and start to learn all about me and how I came there. Not being an expert Japanese linguist, it took some time to explain matters. However, at last the policeman left and I went to sleep.

But I had reckoned without Japanese officialdom. About midnight came two more from the police station, one with gold braid on his arms and cap (a captain at least), the other one supposedly an interpreter but his knowledge of English was worse than mine of Japanese. For an hour we talked and argued. They filled a small book with questions and answers. However, it was settled that after breakfast I was to take ricksha and return via Ishinomaki. Asleep at last.

Being an early riser, I got breakfast. Seeing a barber shop

opposite the hotel went across and had a wash and shave. Made inquiries of the barber about the best and quickest way to get to Ishinomaki. They told me to take ricksha to Ono Mura, get food there, and change ricksha for Ishinomaki. Well, I started after paying the hotel bill.

After being an hour on the road, heard a great hullabaloo behind us. Looking round saw two or more ricksha racing up behind us, two men to each ricksha. Coming closer, saw they contained two officials. Turned out to be the men who had interviewed me at the hotel at midnight. They were gesticulating and halooing for us to stop. Then they started the story and gesticulation that I had thought was settled the night before.

They at first said I must go back to Sendai, which I refused point blank to do. I told them I was to stop at Ono Mura for my midday meal, and there to change rickshas for one to take me to Ishinomaki. It turned out they had telegraphed to the M. B. Company's agent at Oginohama about me and were told the simple story that I was an employee of the M. B. Compay, that I had brought up a tow boat to relieve the one in use at Oginohama, which had to go to Yokohama for repairs, and as I would have to wait three days for the other boat, I had told the agent I would like to go to Sendai and that he had given me the chance to cross the bay in the boat I had brought up.

The agent had telegraphed to the head office of my arrival at Oginohama and that having three days to wait I had gone to Sendai. They answered, stop my going to Sendai as I had no passport. Of course, both the agent and myself were in the wrong as I had no passport, but neither of us thought about a passport.

Anyhow, we got to Ono Mura, where I had the best the landlord could provide me. He was on my side and was tickled to death when he heard how the foreigner, the first he had in his house, had tricked the police. We did not hurry up; I had told the landlord where I was going and to get me a one-man ricksha. The police said I must have two men. I refused unless they paid the extra man. So we started.

When we arrived at the river we had to get a boat to carry us across, the company's office being on the opposite [side]. Seeing us arrive, he thought I was arrested. When he heard the story, he was greatly tickled and more than pleased that I had got through without serious trouble.

After giving us the best he had, I got him to get a boat to take me to Oginohama; I would not go in a boat with the police, nor take them in my boat. So we started, getting to Oginohama about 7 p.m.

One of the company's steamers being in port, I told my boatmen to put alongside the steamer. The police trying to interfere, [I told them] they must do as I wanted them or they would get no money. I got on board and gave them all a surprise when they had heard the story.

Though after their chow time, they soon had a hot meal and something to wash it down. Being tired with my day's travelling, I asked the purser to inform the agent on shore that I was all right, was to sleep on board, and would see him in the morning. . . .

TAKING the relieved steamer back to Yokohama, I was caught in a Southwest gale and had to take shelter in the Choshi River at Inubo-saki. Got in well enough, but leaving, touched some rocks inside the river and did slight damage to the boat's bottom.

When I got to the head office in Tokyo, they had a good laugh at my trip to Sendai without a passport and my trouble with the police.

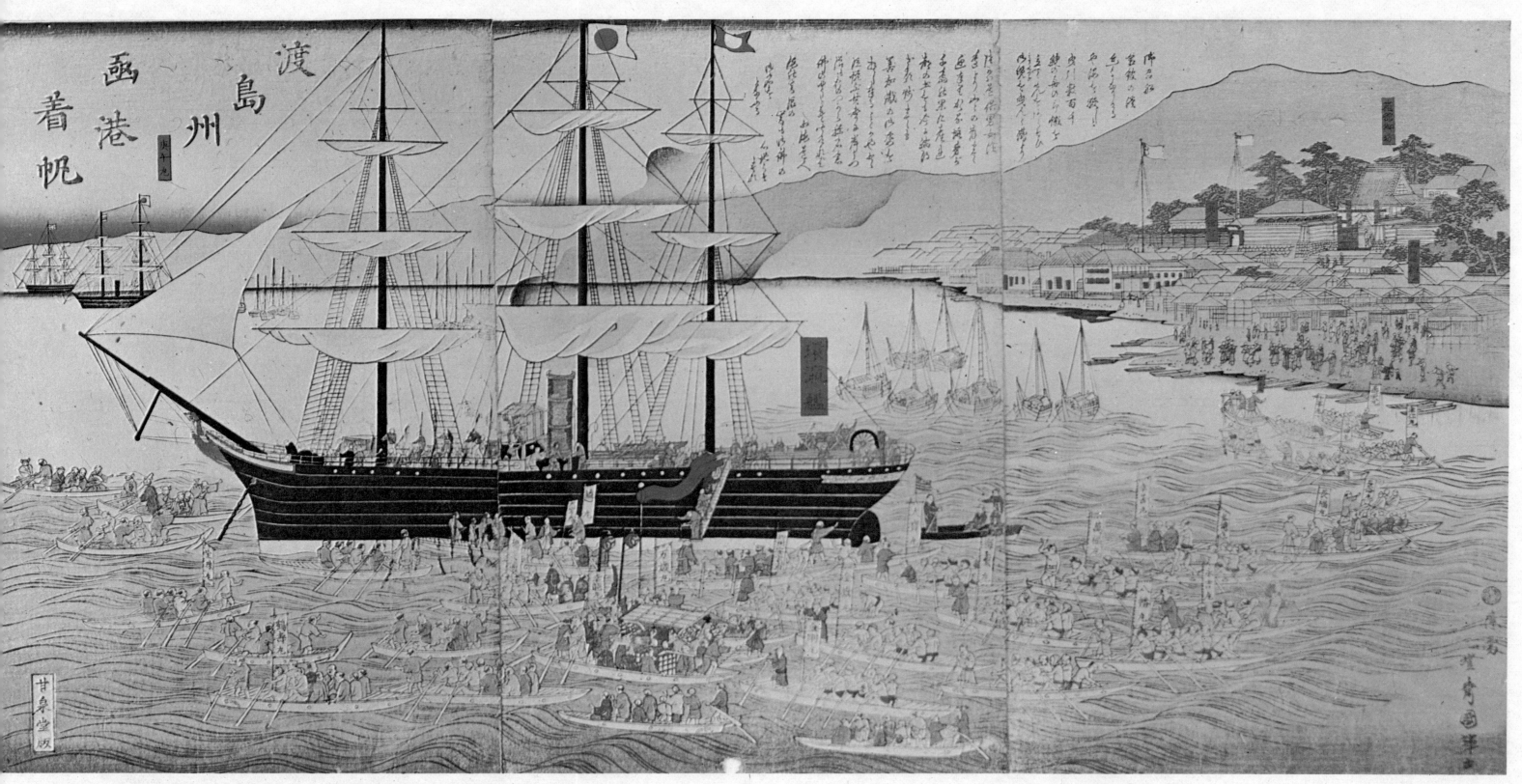

Plate 5: The Kanyei Kan, a Japanese man-of-war, in Hakodate harbor in 1871. The smaller
vessel, on the left, is the *Kogo Maru*. The official residence of the Governor of Hakodate
and the house of Otsuya Seiemon are marked, as is the building of the American Consul
Rice. *(Courtesy of Mr. Carl H. Boehringer.)*

[thirteen]

SALVAGING OFF
FUNAKAWA AND NEMURO

ON THE RESERVE again for some months till wanted in some other expedition. I was wanted either for a wreck or as pilot where no one else had been before. But these jobs only lasted for two or three weeks, then back to the reserve again, drinking or loafing around Yokohama, wasting my health. I dared not leave Yokohama for a day but must be within call.

Next, as far as I can recollect, I was wanted at the head office in Tokyo. On arrival there I was called in to the private office of the foreign heads of the company and was asked what I knew about Funakawa, the port of Akita. One of their big ships had got into Funakawa, which is a bad place to get into if you don't know it.

They showed me the chart used by the captain, in which he had marked some shoals and his bearings of said shoals from the high land east of Funakawa village. I said I did not know of them, but said that I had taken soundings when entering Funakawa. I told them that there were a lot of ridges in the bottom which would make the master of any vessel entering the port for the first time nervous and make him think he had taken the wrong passage in, which he must have done, as I knew nothing of the shoals marked on his chart.

Then I was told to take plenty of warm clothes, the month being November, and that the *Kumamoto Maru*, under Captain Drumond, one of three large ships, was going to load a cargo

{ 129 }

I

of rice at two ports on the west coast. He would land me at Funakawa, then go to the rice ports, load the cargo, then call for me on his way back. I was also told to get the position of the shoals and that he had lost and left two anchors and chains about the place where he got into difficulties.

I mentioned at the head office that it was too late in the year to be able to do anything in boats on the west coast, that they ought to have sent me up in August when the loss happened. They knew that, but said that the Japanese directors insisted that I had to go now. They would write their agent at Funakawa to help me supply anything regarding boats, men, ropes etc. and would see that I was accommodated first class.

I reported to Captain Drumond and asked when his ship was to leave. He said his orders were to leave as soon as I got my clothes on board. His ship had been ready for sea and was only waiting for final instructions about calling at Funakawa and landing me there. So I got my things on board and we started.

CAPTAIN Drumond was a very careful navigator. As I have mentioned before, the sea bottom entering Funakawa was in ridges. In getting into the harbour, the quartermaster at the lead began calling:

'7, 6, 5, 4 ½, fathoms.'

The captain called out after 4 ½ fathoms to stop and go astern.

'No,' I said, 'cast again'.

'5 ½ then 4 ½ fathoms...' and so it went on till we got in to a steady 5 fathoms.

Then I said, 'you can anchor now, we are far enough in.' So

we anchored with 5 fathoms all around, good holding ground.

The captain said he would stop all night; as the weather did not look promising and as he had never been at the ports he was to call at, he would start in the morning. So the mate and I went on shore by the ship's boat. The mate having his shotgun, went over the high land looking for game, with the quartermaster he had brought along. I went the other way to hunt up the company's agent. The mate came back in about two hours bringing four big geese, as much as his man and he could carry.

By this time it was beginning to look like a blow. They just got on board and the boat hoisted up, when the gale broke starting from the eastward, with rain, backing round by S.W. and west, blowing fresh. Looking from the shore in the morning, the steamer seemed to be surrounded by breakers and broken water, leaving no sign of passage into port. However, the steamer was riding safely in deep water. Captain Drumond was surprised at the outlook seaward from his ship.

She stayed two days till the gale finished before leaving, as he could have done nothing towards working cargo at the ports he was bound to. I could do nothing in the work I came to do, so I got on board again and got bearings from the anchorage of the worst breakers, and of the break in the high hill east of the village which was important to me in looking for the place where the chains and anchors were supposed to be lost.

The steamer gone and the weather settling down as much as it was likely to do at that season of the year on the west coast, got two boats and five or six men in each and started out to look for the anchors and chains. They supplied me men that said they knew the spot where the anchors were lost. So we went to the places; but though able to see the bottom clearly, could see nothing of what we were looking for and no trace they had ever been there. This ended the first day's search.

Twice later with different boatmen we went out to different places but found no trace of chains or anchors. The boatmen refused at last to go, saying (as I had told at the head office) that it was too late in the year to go looking for anything on the bottom of the sea; the gales and heavy seas might have covered them up. As I had no people or tools to drag for them, I gave it up. The *Kumamoto Maru* came back. I got on board and we got back to Yokohama.

WHEN the *Kumamoto* got back, they started to discharge her cargo, put on board coal and stores, and she was ordered to leave for Nemuro, Hokkaido. One of their steamers was fast on shore on the rubble shoal north of Cape Noshappu. Captain Drumond wired the head office there were no charts of the strait or approaches to it and refused to go. They wired back:

'Sending Will as pilot.' So he said;

'All right; send Will, will go.' This was all done within forty-eight hours after arrival from Funakawa.

After getting ashore next day, as I knew nothing of what was happening, I went down to the company's sail loft to make out my Funakawa report of the search for anchor and chains. There were wires all over Yokohama. Will was wanted at once at the head office, even the superintendent was looking. The reserve ship was called; Will had not been there; they went to my house; I had left at the usual time in the morning.

Eventually I was found in the sail loft making out my report. Never mind the report, get to the head office; I was wanted quick. Was told about the wreck, was told about Captain Drumond's refusal to go and his reason for it. I was again told to take plenty of warm clothes and blankets and prepare to stop there all winter if necessary.

So I started back to Yokohama, got the clothes I wanted, and reported myself to the captain. The superintendent told me he was also going in the *Kumamoto* to Nemuro and was taking a diver, Jan de Boer, with us. We joined the steamer that night and left for Nemuro.

Approaching Noshappu, the superintendent and Captain Drumond came on the bridge. It being clear weather I was able to let them see two peaks on Kunashiri Island, which, by keeping them clear of Noshappu light house, kept them clear of the reef in the middle of the strait. In thick weather it was risky, but I had gone through in small vessels many times by judging my distance off the lighthouse as I had gone through, almost by instinct.

After passing the lighthouse we were in full view of the wreck, but we did not turn westward here, as there was a large rubble shoal on which the wreck was lying perfectly upright, as if at anchor. I drew their attention to two head lands about half-way between the lighthouse and Nemuro Island. Passing the cape you had to keep the same course till the far head land opened and showed a second point of land; keeping the two points open you cleared the shoal and could steer for Nemuro. Also by keeping certain islands open you could clear the shoal; when you had the lighthouse on the bearing, steer for the strait.

After passing the wreck a mile or two we anchored and low-ered a boat. I was sent in her with the diver and his gear. He was to go round the wreck, look at her bottom and report to me its condition. The superintendent was to follow us in an hour.

We got on board the wreck which, as I have said, looked as if she was lying at anchor. The diver went down, walked round the wreck as if walking on a floor. The water perfectly clear, his head no more than two feet below water when he stood upright. He reported, nothing the matter, and he asked me if I would go in with him and buy the wreck. He would give a report and condemn her.

In the meantime I had been below in the engine and boiler rooms and saw the bottom had risen [she was hogged] and was broken away from the ship's sides, in fact, she could not be salvaged. I said nothing to the diver. The superintendent coming on board, I gave him the diver's report, then asked him to come below and have a look. Like me, he saw she was unsalvable.

Then I was told to get to work and get the windlass and winches adrift from the deck, ready for sending them on board the *Kumamoto*. So we saved what we could, and started for Nemuro to report to the head office. Anchored outside the harbour; too big a ship to get inside the island.

That night it came on to blow from the east; had to put down two anchors and 60 fathoms of chain. A little sea got up; Captain Drumond got anxious and would not let me sleep.

Eventually put on my clothes and went with him to the wheel house, where he kept asking me could we not go here or there to get better shelter. I told him shelter could be found under the islands to the east of the cape, but rather dangerous at night time. He asked about [shelter] under Kunashiri Island, I said by the time we got there, the wind would haul round south, as easterly blows never lasted long, quickly hauling round south to west; and it turned out so. In the morning the wind was off the land; sea going down.

The superintendent was able to land and wire to the head office. Came on board and told us that I was to be landed at the wreck with some men to try and save the boiler, which was a new one. After we got to where we left the wreck, we found the vessel had disappeared in the blow, the boiler only remaining, and it had rolled up on the beach. So my job was finished and there was nothing to do but go back to Yokohama on reserve again.

MY NEXT call from the head office was to join one of the small steamers as pilot. I was to report to Captain Clarke. His vessel was one of the smaller ships but a full powered steamer; could do her 10-11 knots in good weather. She was bound for Shibetsu [the manuscript states 'Sabets'] and another small river on the N.E. coast of Hokkaido to load some salmon as well as bring away any coolies that had been left.

When I got on board to report, the captain was not on board. The mate who had been in the company longer than I, wanted to know what I had come for. I said the captain had orders from the head office and would tell him what my business on board was. When the captain got on board and told him I was sent as pilot, the mate got riled and said he had been in the company longer than I had, and had never had or wanted a pilot before. I told Captain Clarke if this was the way I was received I would go on shore and wire the head office.

'You have had your instructions from Tokyo. Shut this know-all-pup of a mate of yours up or I'll go on shore. Come, send this boaster forward to his work. I will have something to say to him before the voyage is done.'

I must say here that the sandbanks between the highland of northeast Hokkaido and Kunashiri Island are liable to shift yearly with gales and drifting ice from the Okhotsk Sea. The previous year I had been to the Shibetsu River and found the deepest water close to Notsuke Spit, so went same way. But, in sounding this, found certainly less water than that given on the chart. The captain was looking anxious. I said:

'Go on, we will deepen the water directly.'

After anchoring off Shibetsu at dinner the mate began to talk about the difference we found in the soundings and the chart. I explained the reason to Captain Clarke.

(Some years before when in Nemuro, Count Kuroda of Kaitakushi fame had been there in the steamer *Kuroda* and they wanted to go through the Noshappu Strait. They had been twice at the strait but it being the foggy season the captain would not tackle the passage. Coming back to Nemuro, my vessel being in port, he had sent along to Maruhon House where I was living—I suppose they wanted to get back to Sapporo—and had asked about the passage north between Hokkaido and Kunashiri Island. I had told him I had never been north of Nishibetsu, but my chart gave plenty of water; also that the sandbanks between the island were reported as shifting in early spring from winter gales and ice from the Okhotsk Sea. At the same time had said, if [one] got hold of Noshappu light-house [one] always managed to get through the strait.)

WE GOT back safely to Hakodate from Shibetsu. Our cargo and coolies were discharged. They put a cargo of rice or other cargo on board for Otaru.

The mate thinking he had been long enough away from Yokohama, up in cold weather, thought he would try his luck and get a better job. I was asked to fill his place till another man came from Yokohama. I did not like the job as I knew Captain Clarke's ideas of handling his ship entering port.

We started, and it being winter time, got as far as Cape Shirakami. When her nose was pointed round the cape, we met the full blast of the winter gale and sea. Hung on for some time, but the captain finally gave it up and ran back to Hakodate. I had asked him to anchor in the bay half-way back to Hakodate, but no, he would go back two days or more.

In Hakodate the passengers began to growl. We left again, went through the same experience, back again to Hakodate.

This time I rebelled, got on shore, and told the agent I would not go anymore in the ship, fooling around getting nowhere. The agent, a friend of Captain Clarke's, did not like me leaving. Commenced to bluster.

'It is none of your business,' I told him, 'I was sent on board as pilot to take the ship through Noshappu Strait and to Shibetsu River. I did that. The ship came back here safe; my work is done, and as you were short of a mate, I only took his job on to save the company trouble.'

I got on board one of the large steamers, got to Tokyo, reported what I had done, and was told it was intended that I should stay in Hakodate and relieve Captain Clarke of his job. (Had they settled this on the return of the ship from Shibetsu, the steamer would have got to Otaru before this.)

Went on reserve again.

I HAD quite a spell on reserve this time; nothing coming along for my services. My next call, I think, was to take command of one of the three sailing vessels the company had. They were used for carrying coal from Nagasaki to Yokohama. She was the smallest of the three sailers. She had belonged at one time to the Sultan of Turkey. They had taken the machinery out of her and rigged her as a three masted brigantine, i.e. squared-rigged on the foremast. Being yacht-built, she had a fine bottom and sailed fast.

The fun of the story was that her captain had applied for sick leave to go to Hakone Springs. As the sailors were never in a hurry, it generally took two months or more to Nagasaki and back, and the captain I relieved, put off going up to the springs, calculating that at least two months would be taken up on the voyage. The longest part of the voyage was usually getting S.W. to Nagasaki against the Black Current and prevailing winds in the Pacific.

Well, got away from Yokohama with a fair wind that took us out clear off Tokyo Bay to the Pacific without a hitch; then an easterly wind and rain came in and continued four or five days; thick rainy weather, wind fresh, but we could carry our main sails full, some of the lighter ones fast. We saw no sun, ran on dead reckoning.

One morning saw discoloured water. As I have said, we had seen neither sun, moon, nor stars and no land after leaving Iro-saki. The discoloured water we found to be coming out of that bay south of Toi-saki, thus we had come faster than dead reckoning gave us [to believe]. We hauled her south a little and made the land of the northeastern entrance of Van Dieman Strait; ran through the strait, picked up the light house of Satono-misaki, rounded it, and stood up northwest for Naga-saki.

Our easterly wind kept on till within some 60 miles of Nagasaki. Then for a day or two, light and variable wind, to the mouth of the harbour. Wind fell away, calm and we anchored. Then a light breeze came, enough to carry us inside the island; anchored again for a time. Then the usual south-west winds came and away we got; weighed our anchor again, and slid quietly to a berth.

The other two sailing ships belonging to the company were lying in port. It did not often happen that all three sailing ships were in one port together, but this came about by us making the passage in so quick time, and people were surprised to see all three company coal ships in port at one time. The other two ships were loaded and ready for sea next day.

As I have said, the summer winds blew up the harbour during daytime; at night they fell away. Sometimes a light breeze would come off the land, enough to tempt one to get up anchor and try to get out. But it was risky and as the one towboat, a small one, could only take one at a time, the rivalry between the two captains as to who would get the first tow out was keen.

As it was, my friend and myself were dining that night with the owner of the towboat and after dinner, going on board our ships, we heard the pauls of some ship's windlass rattling from well up the harbour. My friend said to me that was old *Kana-*

gawa Maru getting under way. As I have said, the southwest winds died away at night and a light breeze would come off the land, but it was risky.

Anyway, this is what happened: Enough wind had come up to swing the ships head up, and there was a mooring buoy close astern of the *Kanagawa Maru*. The captain made a rope fast to it, hove his anchor up and let his ship swing head down the harbour by the stern rope that he had made fast to the bouy. This was all very clever and he would steal a march on his friend in the other ship.

Having swung round, he made sail on his ship, and slipped his stern rope. But before he got steerage way on his ship, he collided with my ship, doing slight damage; but then ran into a sailing vessel astern of my ship, carrying away her jib-boom and fore-topgallant mast and some of her running rigging. Did not stop but went off on his voyage to Yokohama.

At daylight next morning there was a great to-do. The captain of the damaged vessel reported the collision to the agent at the company's office and to the surveyor in Nagasaki, an American mail-steamer captain, retired.

The company's agent and surveyor came alongside my ship, the surveyor calling out to me;

'Come on Will and let us examine the damage that mad man's ship did last night to the bark astern of you.'

This was the first time I had heard of damage. I knew they had slid along our side carrying away one or two small ropes and thought no more about it. Looking at the ship astern, [I could see] some of the jib-boom stays were hanging loose and something was wrong with the fore-topgallant mast. The surveyor called again:

'Come in the boat Will, you will have to do the climbing. I am too old and you are more of a seaman than I am.' The agent also asked me to come and help assess and settle the damage in behalf of the head office. The other sailing vessel had been properly towed out early in the morning and knew nothing of the collision.

Well, I went on board with the surveyor and agent, did the climbing they wanted. When I had reported what [damage] had been done, it was compared with the captain's own report, then the cost [was figured out]. The captain had an estimate from a Chinese carpenter to put everything as it was before— at so much. The agent and surveyor went on one side, consulted, and agreed it was reasonable; told the captain to go on, the agent would pay the bill. The captain generously did not claim anything for detention. So everyone left satisfied.

Now the fun comes in Tokyo. The account and amount of damage reached the head office from the agent at Nagasaki, by mail steamer, before the coal ship arrived. When she arrived the captain reported at the head office, but made no mention of having collided with another vessel. When he was leaving the office, they stopt him and showed him the surveyor's report.

'Oh, he is an old steamboat man' he said, 'and knows nothing about sailing ship gear; all bosh.'

'You think so—the agent and surveyor may not know much about sailing ships, but here is Will's name signed to it. What have you got to say against Will as a sailor?'

Well, he had to cave in. Then they told him that more haste makes less speed, that he ought to have waited as the other vessel did and been towed out in the morning.

CAPTAIN Ekstrandt never forgave me and as he drew lots of water at the head office he did all he could to hurt me, and succeeded in the end. Captain Ekstrandt was a thorough seaman and a smart one, but he never liked me, like so many other captains in the company. Not many of them were Captain Ekstrandt's equal as a shipmaster, but I knew all of them and where they sprung from, and if I was round, with one or two exceptions, there was no blowing off what they had been or done before joining the company. This was why they did not like to have me on their ships as an officer or have to pilot their ships to places they had never been. As I have said, there were one or two who treated me well, but the exceptions proved the rule. Still, they had to depend on me and knew it.

GETTING back with the sailing ship from Nagasaki we had again good luck. We made the quickest round of any of the three sailing colliers. On landing at Yokohama [I met] some friends, among them the captain I had relieved for the voyage; he had never started for the springs, as he expected I would at least have been a month longer on the voyage. I said I was in luck and could not make the voyage longer to please him.

We went on board to settle up. The money from head office having come, I grabbed the captain's wages as my share. He did not like it, there was a little hitch about the payment, and he thought he had me; but I turned up the apprentice's account, and it was found correct, and he had to apply to the head office for his wages. How it was settled, I don't know. On reserve again.

THIS YEAR I was called upon as pilot some three times to Iturup [Etorofu Island]. With Captain Carew once; here I found that mate whom I had met before with Captain Clarke and he began blattering again about his abilities as a navigator. Captain Carew cut him short and told him he was a child in comparison with me not only in navigation but in knowledge of Japan; [and that he well should] take his hat off to me when on board any ship in Japan.

Another pilot voyage was with Captain Hubbard, also to Iturup Island; as well as a voyage for seaweed. I had never been at the place before, but I had looked into it, of course, as I knew the coast. We got into the place all right, but had trouble when we came to get out again and we had to get a native who told us we had come in the wrong side of the rock and let us out the other side all right, no damage done. So I learned a trick here. I made all together three trips as pilot to Iturup in the four years I was in the M.B. Company. The last time put a top on them all.

I WAS in Hakodate. It was late in the year. Two of their 1000 ton or over steamers had been sent to Iturup Island to bring back the coolies that had been taken there for the season; they came back and reported it was too late. The weather was too bad and they could not get into the places where most of the coolies were.

Well, there were 800 coolies on Iturup that ought to have been brought back and, what was more, there was no food on the island to keep them till spring. So, as the company contract called on them to bring back the men they had taken there, they had to make another attempt. Why they should have picked upon the old middle-sized steamer of 5 or 600 tons is a mystery I cannot fathom. Anyhow, they settled it.

As I said, I was in Hakodate. They brought a letter to me from the head office which read I was to take the steamer to Iturup and bring away the 800 coolies left there. Enclosed was a copy of their letter to the captain of the steamer, which instructed him to take his ship to Hakodate, deliver the letter, get me on board, take his ship out of the harbour, hand her over to me as responsible pilot, and leave her in my charge until the ship returned to Hakodate.

Of course, he was master of the ship, but where or how I went, the ship was at my orders.

Withers, the captain, was a Cockney born and was also a cantankerous individual. He was an older man than me, he said, and from his manner he objected, but his orders were plain: take his ship out of Hakodate harbour and hand her over to me as responsible pilot; when she came back to port I would hand her back to him. Only thing I could see in the order was that they had sent two larger steamers early in the season and failed to get all the coolies, the principal reason for which they had been sent. So why did they send a smaller vessel later in the season, and an older ship and captain than either of two vessels they had sent before? Did they think she might get lost (as I have said she was an old ship) or that by sending me I could handle the small ship better round corners?

Anyhow, they put trust in Old Will; he had helpt them before, and was not a man to give up a job if by any means I could put it through. Well, the long and short was we did get through bringing all the men.

Only my knowledge of the island and the places where the men were located did the job. The purser they sent [was] an old friend (we had been on Iturup together before) and with him any trouble I was likely to have with the captain was cut out.

The purser and I arranged where we were to anchor and send men to Shana, the principal fishing station, where most men were, and round them up. They were to cross the island to the big bay on the south coast of the island. Thus, instead of calling at Shana and small places round it, we would steam up to the N.E. corner, where there would be one big crowd waiting, get them on board; and then steam down the lee side of the island taking all the Shana men and others waiting there in the south bay; then go on to Nemuro and back to Hakodate. This was carried out without a hitch.

After getting the men on board, steaming down the coast, it was blowing a strong northwest. With one exception, it was the oddest I had ever felt at sea. (The other was getting into Cheefoo in January 1861.) I thought my heels were a foot deep. But everything has an end. We got to Nemuro and Hakodate, where I handed my responsibility back to the captain again. We got down to Shinagawa and I went to the head office to report.

With a man like him it was not all smooth running. One time, in his cabin, I had to talk sharp to him and he let fly at me in the face with his fist. Before going on shore to the head office, he begged I would say nothing about the blow he gave me, telling me at the same time I was right in what I had said to him. This ended my Iturup piloting for the M. B. Company.

MY NEXT JOB was [being] put in charge of one of the older

K

boats, laid up wrecked, on the northeast coast of Nambu. This time it turned out to be one of the favoured captains, my old friend Frahm, whom I had the trouble with in Kobe getting the locomotive boiler on board.

He had got married in the interval and had his wife on board with him. On a trip, when he was getting close up to (or thought he was close up to) Tsugaru Strait, the quartermaster had reported a light on shore where no light was supposed to be. The captain had ordered the helm to starboard and had run towards the light, taking it for the light on Shiriyasaki. How all on board could have been deceived is still [a mystery], but so it was! She had run on shore some twenty or more [miles] south of Shiriyasaki.

One of their first class steamers outside the mail boats (in fact, she was sister ship to the mail boat wrecked at Shimonoseki) was ordered to get ready. She was commanded by one of their No. 1 captains, like the one whose ship was on shore. This time not only the outside lot were to go, but all the head foreign employers in the head office: the superintendent; the captain; four or more engineers on reserve; boiler makers (my friend MacGregor at their head); carpenters and timber; the sailmaker and his crew, with canvas and oakum to make soft patches; besides boatmen, of course.

I was among the crowd; in fact, the foreign manager, Mr. Krebs, told the superintendent that I was to go; and the captain of the steamer insisted, as his mate was tired, having been busy getting all on board ready for sea, that I should keep his mate's watch. The superintendent came and asked me to do so as everyone on board was supposed to help what they could. I said yes, though there were other reserve officers on board that could have kept the watch. Captain Walker insisted I should take the job; he would go to the manager if I refused.

I soon found out his reason for insisting my being appointed. He knew nothing about the place we were going to. As things turned out, the ship was running along a safe distance off the coast and, while all the crowd were on deck looking, a black rock lying close to the land appeared like a ship on shore. The bosses were all on the poop looking and the other crowd were on the forecastle head, shouting and saying that that was her. Others with better heads said it was a rock. I had turned out and gone forward. As they could not agree, the bosses aft raised the cry;

'Where is Will?'

'His watch below,' they were told.

'Oh, get him up!'

In the meantime I was forward. The cry again was to come aft. By this time I had made up my mind that it was the Black Rock of Tomari Mura and not the wreck; so I told them so.

Some years before I had been close in that shore looking if there was any chance to get firewood to take me to Hakodate as I had been in a typhoon and was short of coal. Sailing close in shore I had come up to the rock.

After this we steamed along the coast but could not pick up the wreck. So it was arranged we should go on to Hakodate and get definite instructions as to where the wreck was: we lay there all day.

Got started at midnight, reached the wreck early next day, and anchored over a mile off shore: lowered boats and took workmen on board. Also arranged to get some large boats and took a small boiler to start a pump.

The fore hold was perfectly dry, but the after part was smashed up. As the wreck had a deep tank aft which did for either cargo or water ballast, the boilermaker, MacGregor, was trying to fix a pump in the hatchway. He tumbled off the beam he was trying to fix into the tank. There was no one near him and he could not get out without help. The tank being some 18 or 20 feet deep, he dived down and seeing daylight in the ship's side, he made for it, got through the big hole, came up alongside and up the gangway. That evidence was enough she was not worth saving, but we held on till next day when some wind and sea came looking ugly.

The superintendent called me to go to Captain Walker and get the best boat on the ship. There was some trouble about letting me have the best boat. The superintendent came along and told him to give me any boat I wanted. I took the sail maker's boat crew and got her at the gangway; got in her myself to steer; got the head manager and the superintendent in the boat and was told to go to the wreck.

Under the lee it was quite smooth. They got on board, looked all round, came back to the gangway, called me up, and I walked round with them again. Came aft and stood talking, then asking me my opinion. I said it would be labour and money lost to try to do anything to her; the first east gale would break her up.

'That's settled then; let's get on board and back to Tokyo.'

Back again on board the old steamer I was looking after.

I HAD QUITE a spell [on reserve], then I was called to go mate temporarily for a voyage to Miyako on the northeast coast. This a favour asked by the captain. Captain Diffettson was a Dane, a married man, and drew a lot of water at the head office with Mr. Krebs, his countryman. Hitherto she had carried two Japanese officers, but the captain had never been in any of the ports on the northeast coast.

Miyako being poorly sheltered from east winds, he asked for me to go the trip. I had been having a good time and for the first time did not like the job I was going to. I had an inward feeling there would be trouble over it, which turned out true.

I had been having a good time with the boys who came to see me before leaving; lots of whisky drunk. When it came to be my watch, I was not fit to keep it. However, I went on the bridge, spoke to the captain, who could see I was worse for liquor and could not be trusted. Instead of sending me to my room, he left me with a junior officer. Anyhow, I lost command of myself, started to go to my cabin.

As if a trap had been laid for me, two bunker hatches had been left off. Staggering along sick to my room, I tripped and fell down some six feet on top of the coal. Not being able to get up by myself, I had to get help: a strange place and condition for the chief officer on watch to be found in. However, I got to my room, lay down on my settee and by daylight had got rid of the whisky.

But my head felt worse than after any of my previous drinking bouts. Probably the position I found myself in made it worse; knowing I had given the crowd to whom Captain Diffettson belonged the very handle they were waiting for to get me out of the company. Certainly this was the first and only time I put myself in such a position. It was a bad one, and no one knew better than I did how bad it was being the worse for liquor and leaving the bridge.

When I got sobered up I went and apologized to the captain, but he made no comment about it to me. Thinking the more what kind of report he could send in, I may state here that nothing had happened to the ship. Arriving at Miyako he asked me about the best anchorage which I showed him, still making no comment on last night's exploit.

We left on our way back to Yokohama. The captain had told the engineer that he was to report me; he asked the captain if he had told me he was to report me.

'No,' he said.

The Engineer told him he should tell me and give me a chance to put something in on my own side.

'No,' he said.

Of course the engineer told me this.

When I got back to Yokohama I was sent back to my old ship again. So I made up my mind I would write to the head office acknowledging my having been the worse for liquor and having left the bridge while on watch, and the captain making no comment on it during the voyage and letting me go on with my duty as if nothing unusual had happened, then telling the engineer that he had made out a report he was to send to the head office without saying anything to me or giving me a chance of saying anything on my side if I wanted to. This looked like the captain of older standing.

Many of the captains in the company did not like me because the company made use of my knowledge of Japan, especially Hokkaido and the islands, [in their behalf,] sending me as nurse or pilot. Some of them were really pleased to have my assistance, others pretended they knew all about the places they were bound to. But when the test came they were always anxious to have me on the bridge with them. This of course, was as it should be, as I was the man sent by the head office.

I made a great mistake in writing to the head office. I met Howe a year afterwards, No. 2 foreigner in the company. He stopt me and said the people that write letters to head office should know how to dot their i's and cross their t's. This had brought about my dismissal, not the captain's report. I learned after, that really had been the case.

fourteen

WORKING FOR THE
MITSUI BUSSAN KAISHA

OUT OF A JOB, I went on shore. Going along the creek to my house, I met Mr. Killdoyle standing in front of his place, No. 61. He asked me what I was doing on shore at that time of day. I told him I was out of the company and was looking for a job.

'Do you mean it?'

'Yes,' I said.

Then he told me that he and D. Robertson had bought the barque *Samara* that was on shore (at Omae-saki), that he had a dozen men from the crowd that is to be found loafing on Yokohama pier, as well as one or two officers that had been in M. B. Company ships. One was the German Captain Fulert, in charge, but they did not seem to get along with him.

He had asked Captain Stedman, who also had left the company, to go down and boss the job, but Captain Stedman said he was going to another job.

Would I go? 300 [yen] a month and found—500 if I got her off and up to Yokohama. I said, yes.

'When could I go?'

'In two or three hours.'

'Tonight?'

'Yes.'

So it was settled.

Got down next morning. Found her well up on the sandy

beach. Ship all taunt; masts and yards, ballast in her; sails unbent, but most of the running gear aloft. One thing they had done, they had laid out over 100 *fths* of cable chain but had not attempted to put any anchors to the chains, and I found the chains had been all scattered along the beach by the sea. So I started to lift all the chains. Got two anchors and all the chains laid out to deep water as far as we could; brought the end of the chains on board to the windlass and hove tight. Sent the topgallant masts down on deck.

Then started heaving the ballast out, leaving as much in as we thought the ship would need to stand up with. After all the above was done and chains to anchors kept hove tight, there was nothing to do but wait for a swell coming in from sea to move the ship.

As we had hove out half the ballast, I counted with all the cable chain and anchors laid out we had lightened her over two feet or more; at least we had done all we could do without more help, i.e. coolies for digging away the sand. Mr. Killdoyle agreed to wait and see the effect of what we had done.

We had not to wait long. A breeze from the S. W. came away, not too strong but enough to send in a swell that moved the ship in her bed. Then all hands got excited. The windlass was manned and hove up on, as it had never been before, as the men were all anxious to get back to Yokohama. Deep sea lead was over the side, and Mr. Killdoyle went aft with another lead and line in his hand; as well, we kept points of land to watch by—like the job I had with floating the Russian gunboat off a sandy beach.

She had moved in to her bed tightly, but that gap widened and kept on widening; then she began to slide a foot, then more, all the time we were keeping the chain like a fiddle string. Then we quickly found we had her in hand and she swung round to the wind; she was afloat. This was afternoon.

The next thing was for a steamer to tow us; we had the sails on board but having hove out the best part of the ballast, we were afraid to put up sails. Mr. Killdoyle got on shore and went to the nearest telgraph office he could find. Wired to Yokohama and ports along the coast for help. Eventually a small coasting steamer from Yokkaichi came along and took us in tow till we got round Rock Island.

It was slow work, although we bent and set some staysails. But when we turned round the island and headed for Tokyo Bay, we bent and set the main and foresails, and as the wind freshened the tow had all she could do to keep ahead.

When the news got to Yokohama that the *Samara* had been floated, the people along the shore at Yokohama were all cheering Killdoyle for his big job getting his ship off. When the ship appeared in tow after passing Kannon-saki, some steam launches put out from Yokohama to meet the ship and have a look at the damage she was supposed to have sustained. Among the first to get on board was Captain MacDonald, Lloyd's surveyor, and when he got to the top of the gangway and saw me there to meet him his first words were;

'Hiloh (hello) what are you doing here?' I said I had been down helping Mr. Killdoyle to get his ship afloat. He laughed:

'That explains much of what was puzzling people in Yokohama. Well, since you are here I want you to go round with me to have a look at the damage.'

'Why? Unless there may be some paint off her bottom through hauling off the sand beach, everything as far as I have seen about her appears as if she had just come out of dry dock.'

'Oh no,' he said, 'the report was her back was broken'.

'The butt ends of the deck planks will tell us that,' I said, 'I had not thought of looking for anything so serious; ship was perfectly tight and, as you will see below, there is not even a crack in the cement washing in the hold as far as I can see.'

Captain Varnum had come with the surveyor. After the three of us had gone over the ship on deck looking at the butt ends and down below—they came to the conclusion that the whole story was a lie and [a case of] complete dereliction of duty and desertion of the ship.

The late captain of the ship had got off with his story that the ships back was broken and that she was not worth the expense of refloating, if that could be done at all. The captain, I heard by the time his ship was refloated and in Yokohama again, was already half way to his home. When Lloyds' surveyor reported his survey, a telegram was sent to stop the captain and return him to Yokohama. What they made of this second naval court, if I heard, I was not interested, since I was paid some 100 odd yen for my 10 or 12 days work and the 500 yen for getting the ship afloat and bringing her to Yokohama, though that was not my contract: only to get her afloat.

NOW as my luck would have it, I was paid in the Oriental Bank, supposed to be the No. 1 Bank in Yokohama at that time. So instead of carrying the 500 yen to the Hong Kong Shanghai Bank, I left them on deposit in the Oriental Bank.

After knocking about a week or more I thought of having

a look at Shanghai. So I wrote up to the M. B. head office and asked them for a passage in one of the mail boats to Shanghai in a day or two. They wrote me to go on board the steamer leaving next day, that they had written the captain to give me a first class passage. Paid a visit to the mail boat, saw the captain and he told me it was settled. So I packed up and left for Shanghai.

When I arrived there, the first man I met was Captain Black of the *Hideyoshi*, belonging to the Mitsui Bussan Kaisha. After telling him I was looking for a job, he said his mate was wanting to leave. In the meantime the news had reached Shanghai that the Oriental Bank had stopt payment and closed its doors. So here I was in Shanghai and all my money was in that bank; so I got on board the first boat and got back to Yokohama; found I would have to wait some time before things were settled in the bank.

Second day in Yokohama I received a telegram: come to Shanghai at once as there was a job open, if I cared to take it. Made arrangement with an old shipmate, Donald the Sailmaker, to look after my interests in the Oriental Bank, and got back to Shanghai.

THE JOB was not much. Captain Black asked me to go mate with him in the *Hideyoshi Maru* till something better turned up; all right it was work. I made two voyages as mate. Then Captain Black thought he was sick or tired and asked the Mitsui Bussan Kaisha agent at Kuchinotsu to let him stop behind for a trip and put me in command. That was agreed upon.

The officers and engineers did not like the shift; I had been less than a month in the ship and they knew nothing of my abilities to take charge.

As luck would have it, we tumbled into the tail end of a typhoon before we got as far as the Goto Islands. The weather looked bad, so I put the helm up and put for Nagasaki. Entering Nagasaki we found two or three Russians also putting back. Getting inside the islands, we anchored. Did not go up to the town as the harbour was full of ships.

We lay all that night and next day. Did not report our lying there, which caused a big commotion in Kuchinotsu, our arrival in Shanghai being two days later than usual.

On our arrival at Shanghai the agent there was much surprised to find that I had brought the steamer across and asked anxiously whom I had taken as pilot. He was pleased to hear that no pilot was necessary for any ship I was in charge of, as I had been in and out of Shanghai for over twenty years as officer and captain, mostly of sailing ships which were worse to handle than steamers in the river.

Cargo discharged, got back to Kuchinotsu, found the captain was still ailing and having leeches stuck on his neck. So we were loaded and left again.

This time at Shanghai was pay time; so I paid all the others, took the captain's and my own to Kuchinotsu, gave the captain his share for the one voyage he had made, and kept the captain's wages I had made as master. Captain did not like this but I stuck to it; this got him well quick. Next voyage he returned in command.

AT THIS TIME, besides the two steamers *Hideyoshi* and *Yoritomo*, the Mitsui Bussan Kaisha had two sailing barks in the coal trade between Kuchinotsu and China; one was called the *Comassie*. The captain of the *Comassie* was a stranger to the East and did not get along well with the Japanese and their ways. In fact, he was a little negligent in his business from not being used to any one but his own countrymen. I believe he had said that he wanted to leave, but the quandary was where to get another master for the vessel as sailing-ship master's at that time were not plentiful: any man with a master's certificate wanted to get into steam.

Well, it went around among office and shipping that I was an old sailing-ship master. By this time Captain Black of the *Hideyoshi* thought I knew enough about him and his ways, so he started the racket that I should be put in command of the *Comassie*. All hands being agreeable, I was put in command of her.

This caused quite a stir among the other captains in the company. They had hitherto enjoyed an easy time, starting when it suited them, at times half a day, and certainly never at night ready for sea. As far as I was concerned, if wind and tide permitted, I always left either Shanghai or Kuchinotsu. This was always my way, however or wherever I served. The other captains had to follow suit and did not like it.

THERE HAD BEEN two or three [Japanese] apprentices in the *Comassie* for two or more years before I was in [command of] her. (The elder of the two, in fact both of them, served later as mate and second mate of the *Comassie*.) When I left and joined the *Hideyoshi* [again?], they followed me there. When I got command of the *Tsukushi Maru*, I got them there again.

The company began to think that we foreigners had been long enough in the service, since some of their Japanese officers held master's certificates. (My chief mate in the *Tsukushi*, who had been apprentice in the *Comassie* with me, held an English master's certificate as well as Japanese).

We were in Hong Kong and after discharging our cargo, instead of returning to Japan, the agent took a Chinese charter and we were sent to Saigon, there to load a cargo of rice and bring it to Hong Kong. Having a spare mate on this voyage, I left my Japanese mate behind at his request and with the agent's sanction. He went to a navigation school for a week or more, not that he wanted much cramming, as he had passed through the Japanese examination previously, but merely to learn formal English.

When we arrived back from Saigon, found he had gone through without a hitch, got his certificate, he being one of the first, if not the first, Japanese to get an English certificate in Hong Kong.

Clearing my vessel at the harbour master's office I begged for a few minutes' talk with him, and asked him if my mate got through all right. The harbour master said:

'Well, I have had a number of people before me for examination, but your Japanese young man certainly went through with flying colours. There was not a scratch on any of his papers nor the least hesitation in his verbal answers to questions asked him.' I thanked him for the trouble of seeing me, and left him well pleased with his report.

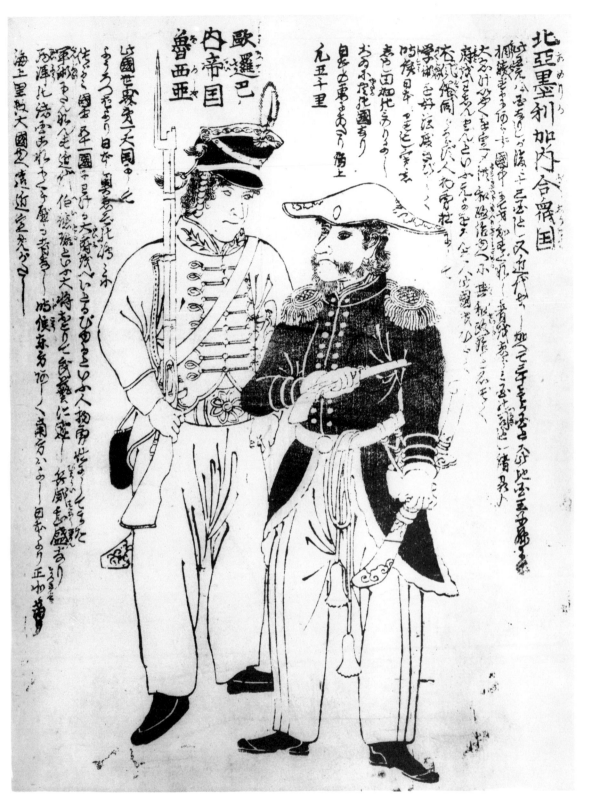

Plate 6: A black-and-white woodblock news broadside depicting a Russian (left) and an American (right). The description of the United States notes: 'The throne of the country is not handed down to the descendants of a king, but the government of the country is placed into the hands of wise men chosen from among the people.' Concerning Russia the broadside states: 'This is the greatest country in the world .... The people are valorous and are well trained in the military art.' *(Courtesy of Carl H. Boehringer.)*

So the company thought it was time to let the Japanese make good what they had learned from foreigners, not only as deck officers but also as engineers. I was relieved by my mate in the *Tsukushi*, sent to Kuchinotsu, there to await orders, on pay all the time.

AFTER BEING on shore a month or more, they wired from Shanghai to come there and bring my English certificate with me. I knew they had two vessels there still under the Japanese flag, one an English steamer they had bought at that port and my old ship the *Comassie*. When I got to Shanghai, I found they had got the steamer transferred back to the English flag, but the British consul would not retransfer the *Comassie* back to her old flag. As things were getting serious with the Japanese in Shanghai [1895], the people in the office were anxious to get back to Japan, the vessel was handed over to the agency of Dunn & Company there. So I was left [with] the ship still there, living on shore at the Oriental Hotel.

After about a month kicking about during the dog days, the American consul agreed to transfer her to the American flag. I had previously sailed the *Maggie Lauder* under the American flag, so I was introduced to the American consul as the Captain of the *Comassie*. After looking me up and down the consul remarked, you look as like an American as I do.

The trouble came when I wanted to clear the ship I had, to ship a foreign crew for Hong Kong. I had wanted to clear via Guam, which would have left me clear to go any where I wanted, but the consul insisted that he would only clear the ship for Hong Kong via Foochow.

L

We got cleared and towed out from Shanghai. Without saying anything to agents or consul, my intention was to steer for Japan. When we arrived at Nagasaki I had trouble with the American consul, as the Shanghai clearance called for our going to Hong Kong via Foochow, and I had brought the ship to Nagasaki against the consul's clearance.

I put it this way before the consul: the ship was in ballast; there was nothing in the ship to cause me to carry the ship some thousand miles away from her home port, putting her owners to great expense, etc.

Well, the ship was in Japan and even if the M. B. Company had asked me to take her to China again, I would have refused.

When things were settled with the American consul at Nagasaki, we were ordered to go to Moji, there load a cargo of coal for Shinagawa, Tokyo. Previously I had discharged all the foreign crew I had shipped in Shanghai, and the Japanese captain and crew which had left the vessel in Shanghai at the outbreak of the [Sino-Japanese] war had been put on board again. Still I was kept on to represent the American flag, and the Mitsui Bussan Kaisha, of course, looked to me as captain of the *Comassie*. Moreover, without apology I will say, the Japanese could not have taken the bark to Moji through the steamer track.

We were some 10 or 12 days getting to the west entrance to the Inland Sea.

The Japanese captain had telegraphed for a pilot to meet the ship at the entrance of Shimonoseki Strait. I was surprised when the man came on board, and asked the Japanese who he was and why I was not told before leaving Nagasaki.

'As far as I know,' I said, 'I know as much about the straits as most pilots and as for handling the bark *Comassie* in tide waters, I know more about the job than any foreign or Japanese pilot is likely to know.'

So the pilot was sent on shore with a letter to the agent of the Mitsui Bussan Kaisha to pay the pilot a small sum as he had been on the lookout for some days for the ship.

We got to Moji all right, anchored at a loading berth; were loaded and started through the Inland Sea with a full cargo for Shinagawa. In the sea many steamers passed us with foreign pilots on board. They wondered at seeing a bark flying the American flag working through the sea [without a pilot's flag showing]. They all soon found out who the skipper was. Afterwards in meeting in the sea, the pilots would have a joke: hold up the end of a rope as much as to say 'do you want a tow?' Well, we always got along without help.

WE MADE some three or four voyages between Moji and Shinagawa. I don't know whether the ship was paying or not, but arriving in Yokohama one trip, the manager from Tokyo came on board and told me they had sold the *Comassie*, and I was to go to the American consulate with him to hand over the ship to the new owners.

After that, we travelled to Tokyo together. He told me, as they were changing all the foreigners for Japanese in their ships, he was sorry to say they had no more work for me. Of course, I had expected this for some months; they had written me to that effect. He mentioned that as I had been over eleven years in their service and given them every sign of competency, they would like to help me in any way they could.

Besides paying what was due me, they gave me a bonus of ¥1,000 for every year I had been in their employ. I must say, the Mitsui Bussan Kaisha treated me better than any other company I had ever served in Japan or elsewhere.

[fifteen]

STEVEDORING IN NAGASAKI

MY NEXT JOB was stevedoring in Nagasaki. I was well paid; good quarters. The boss was an old friend of mine. I knew the work better than any and we had plenty to do. He had three different gangs of coolies. At least two of the gangs knew me well; they had been at the job for years with the original boss who had started the stevedoring business at Nagasaki some twenty years before. He was a particular friend of mine and I used his house when in Nagasaki as if I had a right to it.

But the present boss had a Japanese wife and she had a Japanese friend who was employed in the office. The friend had started a third gang of coolies who were employed at times on cargoes like general cargo or kerosene oil.

There was usually no objection among the coolies to work, but when it came to a cargo of Cardiff coal for the British Navy there was always hanging back among the three gangs. The boss happened to be away at the hot springs for a week. A coal ship for the Navy came along and it happened to be the turn of this new gang to discharge the coal. The Boss being away, they went to his wife and said it was not their turn. I called the other gangs and they said it was that gang's turn. So I told them to do it or they would get no other job.

They went [to it], but when the boss returned, his wife and her fancy man, the head of the gang, had a whole night's talk with him before I knew he had come back, and as they did not like me they got it into the boss that I favoured the other gangs. So there was trouble.

I told him that at his request I came to help him in his work and did not take orders from his Japanese or any other man. This was the first trouble. Of course, I was afloat most of the time and could not be round to see or hear what was going on.

Eventually it came to his being unable to face me. He told his clerk to write me a letter saying I was to leave at the end of the month. In the interim he had asked another captain, who like me had been discharged from the Mitsui Bussan Kaisha, who wrote and told him:

'If Captain Will cannot get along with you, I could not, as Nagasaki's report said Will was the best man he ever had or was likely to get.'

In the meantime he had written to another man and he got sick; could not come. So he wrote to me asking me to come back, which I refused.

A stevedore in Kobe telegraphed for me to join him in Kobe. I went and was told by an old friend there on my arrival that the job would not suit me. However, I tried it for a month, but here again the Japanese wife and the cook ran the cargo boats and I could not get boats. So I told the boss that I could not stop after the end of the month.

I returned to Nagasaki to settle about my hotel shares, tried to sell them, but there were no buyers, so gave Constable Lawrance my power of attorney to act for me regarding the shares. As the great rush for Klondike was started, I made up my mind, as I had never been on the west coast of America, to see what British Columbia was like. And made one of the hundreds of fools in that Klondike rush.

[*sixteen*]

OFF TO THE
KLONDIKE GOLD RUSH

HAVING some business to settle with the Mitsui Bussan
Kaisha at Yokohama, where all my money had been transferred
from the Shanghai office, I packed my clothes and went to Yokohama, settled up with the Mitsui Bussan Kaisha. Drew what
money I wanted and ran up to Hakodate for a day or two to
see after my affairs there.

Back to Yokohama. Changed ¥1,500 into American money,
took a steerage passage on the Pacific Company Steamer
Pathon and left in her for Victoria, B.C. [*ca.* 1898].

When I arrived there the town was alive with people waiting to get away to the Klondike gold fields. As I had brought
money with me and there was no need to rush, although shipping was scarce, and it would be over a month or more before
any one would get a chance to leave for Skagway, the nearest
port to the overland route to Klondike, I roved about the
locality.

One of the white-funneled steamers came in from Japan. The
captain met me one day; he was an old friend of mine. He was
in trouble. His 2nd mate had been shanghaied and he had to sail
next day for Skagway; would I not help him? As it was still
too soon—being dead winter, the rush would not commence
for a month or more—would I not make one trip, to finish his
charter?

As I hated being idle, waiting, I went with him for the

voyage and well pleased I was with my trip. Went first to Vancouver and, coming back, called at the coal mines; took in coal and left for Skagway, calling at the American customs stations on the line between British America and American Alaska.

We had two pilots on this trip, and being 2nd officer on the ship I had a chance to see something of the inner passages between the islands. Was well pleased as in all my forty-five years experience I had never seen anything so really grand as some of the passages were. I knew the Japan Inland Sea, which I had been often through (in fact, always piloted my own ships through them sailing or steam).

As every one knows, the Japan Inland Sea is pretty, but the inner passages in Northwest America were grand. Fancy running for miles between two high lands over a thousand feet high. To look at them from the ship one would think he could throw a stone from one side to the other; and the land so thickly covered with fir trees from the water edge to the top, one could not see through them. The finest sight I have ever seen in my travels. It seemed as if the ship was in a canal.

Talking with the captain about the Japan Inland Sea—he also had been through the sea often—I said this beats the Inland Sea. He said the pilots had told him they would let him see something he had never seen the like of before, where the water was so many feet higher at the upper than the lower level and the water runs with a rush.

I happened to be on watch. The captain had me called up and I was certainly surprised to see how the ship was handled by the pilots. Of course, when the ship got down to the level, the water was mixed. Speak about an overfall! But I never could think of the rush we had down it. Of course, the rudder was no use when we got to the bottom, but the pilots knew and handled the engines well. In fifteen or twenty minutes we were out of the mixture and going along all smooth.

We got back to Victoria all right and my contract was finished, so I went to the shipping office to sign off and get paid for my trip. The captain wanted me badly to stay on, but I told him I came here to go to the Klondike or as near thereto as I could get. So I went to the hotel again.

HERE I picked up with some Australian miners who had come to live at the hotel. They wanted to make a party of four and asked me if I cared to join them. I told them I knew nothing about mining. They said that did not matter; they would rather have a man who knew nothing about mining, especially as I was an old sailor, a handy man about boats or any ropes, as we would have a long passage to make down the river to Klondike.

Among our stores we bought a boat and necessary gear for the river passage. The boat was put up with screw nails; [could be] taken to pieces, which we saw done, and packed in a bundle to save freight and handling without breakage. Stores we pooled equally together and bought in a lump; clothes, each one bought what he wanted and paid for. All of us bought clothes. As the other three were from Australia they had to buy clothes to suit Klondike; I also had to buy underwear to suit the cold weather. In time we got everything together.

For a start got a passage to Skagway in a steamer, crowded in every corner with all kinds of people. We got to Skagway, landed there, had to go through the American customs routine landing on American soil. Every one was taxed to the utmost as usual with people who had brought money to throw away in their hurry to get to the gold fields.

I wish I could explain all we saw and went through, the folk we saw on the road and how they got along, how and what they carried, i.e. arms for protection. Not alone men but women. I had seen pictures of the mountaineers of the Balkans in their fighting or marauding dress; their belts and breasts loaded with knives, pistols and shot belts. How they were able to travel with all the gear they had about them! Even cripples walking with crutches! Some entertainers such as jugglers, slight-of-hand men, dancers carrying banjos, and others—all trying to get money out of the crowd that were making for the gold fields.

When we started from Skagway I had put on a suit I had bought for Klondike winter wear. It was guaranteed wind and water proof. Now as we still had to travel up the dry bed of a stream full of large boulder stones and rocks and the day was fairly warm, sun shining, and being unused to such roads, with the wind proof clothes I had on I got wringing wet with sweat. When we halted for the night at a shack on the road I was not only tired out, but, as our clothes and stores had been handed to the Overhead Wire Transport Company to be delivered at the White Pass in British territory, could get no chance of shifting my wet, sweaty clothes. So I began to feel that I had undertaken to do more than a man of my age (then 58 years old) who had been some 40 years in ships on the China and Japan coasts, where we were used to the best kinds of food and service.

In the shack we stopt for the night, the only food obtainable was pork and beans. In fact, [this was] the only food to be got on the road; it turned me sick to look at it. Being a sailor I could eat and enjoy any kind of food, but the travelling over stones in the dry river bed, clothed as I was for the first time in my life, I could not look at food. I got into a bunk in which was a straw mattress, or what looked like one, with my sweaty clothes on. There was no place to dry them. In the morning, though tired, I did not feel rested, but had to get ahead, as the crowd following us had also to be put up and we had to get out and make room for them.

Still due for a climb up to what was called the White Pass, which had to be crossed before we got into the Yukon River Valley, we were leaving the shack we had slept at, where we had pork and beans for breakfast, warmed up from what was left of yesterday's cooking. There was a woman belonging to the shack and she, seeing I could not look at the warmed up mess, got me a cup of coffee and some bread she had made for herself. I managed to drink the coffee, put the bread in my pocket, and we started to climb over the snow for the pass.

We stopt for a midday meal at another shack or halfway house. The same food: pork and beans warmed up. Here we were abreast of what they called the Snares. The story was told that on the opposite side of the river some 50 or 100 of the early Klondikers had camped at the foot of the steep snow-covered bluff hill. An avalanche of snow had came down from the hill up on them and buried them and their stores. Some Indians had come along and had tried to get at the bodies and stores but failed. Nothing they were able to do brought anything in sight. So there they lay, the bodies and stores, till doomsday. In climbing up the pass we bared our heads in respect to the dead lying under the snow.

Some enterprising Klondiker had made steps in the steep snow-clad wall of the pass and had cut resting places about every twenty steps. This enabled people to get to the top of the pass easy. Of course, climbers had to pay for using the steps, some 10 cents if I remember right. Anyhow, they paid the step-makers.

On reaching the top of the pass, we were confronted with the Canadian blue ensign and two Canadian Northwest police, fully armed, guarding the pass. There was a shack close too, where the guards were staying. Here everyone had to stop and report, which we did.

As it was now getting dark we had to look out for food and shelter for the night. I got into a canvas tent, but it was a leaky old tent and to crown all, it came on to rain and the rain came through, and when I woke up I found the hammock I was sleeping in with two or three inches of water in it, my clothes all wet and no change of clothes.

As we had to keep moving to make room for others, we started early in the morning to slide down the other side of the pass in heavy snow. I was in fevered condition and started eating snow to quench my thirst. This made me worse; when we got to the foot of the pass and got into a tent I lay on a hard rock for a bed. I was in such a fevered state that though lying on the ground, my body shook so that the other people could not sleep and wanted to know what was the matter. Got through the night but felt bad.

We started in the morning; got to Lake Lindermere before dark. Here we were to stay and put our boat together, get all our stores collected and make ready for our voyage down the Yukon River to Klondike.

At the lake we and some hundred others, all bound down the river, got our tents up, started to put our boats together. Quite a town sprung up all round us. Gamblers, quack doctors, sing-song dancing houses, all that kind of people turned up, all bound the same way.

I would have enjoyed the thing had I been well, but I got worse and my friend got round and found a quack doctor. He took me in for two days, but I woke up one night and found them fingering about me under the bed clothes. I had a belt round my waist; in it were some 400 gold dollars. Next day my friend came to see me and I told him what had happened; they had tried to get me to sleep by putting some mixture in my mouth. So my friend took me back to the camp. By this time I was perfectly helpless. This lasted some two or three days.

At last it was settled I should get back to the nearest place where there was a doctor. This was Skagway. There was no one going back, everyone was bound to Klondike, and I was so helpless that some one had to be found to take care of me if I expected to get back alive. Luckily a Salvation Army man came along, who was going to Skagway on Salvation Army business, and he would be glad to see me back to a doctor. So my friend settled with me for my share of the outfit by cheque on a bank at Victoria.

My Salvation Army friend seemed to know what was wanted, having traveled the road before. Next morning he had a man with a sleigh and four dogs ready to take me up to the pass. Making me and my clothes fast on the sleigh, we started, getting to the pass early in the afternoon. My friend discharged the man, his dogs and sleigh, borrowed another sleigh and making a drag of my clothesbag we slid easily down on the other side of the pass.

Coming to some shacks below the snow, we put up in one of them for the night. Next morning my Salvation Army friend got a horse, put me on its back, walking ahead. Leading it, he kept it clear of boulders in the dry river bed. We got down in the afternoon to the sea, crossed the bay in a boat to Skagway, got into one of the so-called hotels that had sprung up in Skagway.

Here my friend found another Salvation Army man, who was located at that place, and asked him to call a doctor at once. He returned in quick time, bringing Dr. Moore, an Irish American, pleasant-faced gentleman, that looked his profession and proved himself to be what he looked.

After examining me all over and hearing where I had come from and how I had come, he burst out with:

'You must be either Scotch or Irish. There is no other countryman that could have come through what you have today in the condition you are in.'

He got me fixed up and settled in bed. The Salvation Army friend that brought me from Lake Lindermere had to go back there, but he got the friend we met at Skagway to take his place. So after settling with him (all he would take was some clothes, etc., I had no use for) he and the other knelt down and offered up a prayer for my health, rose up, thanked me, and left.

As the doctor said, I was in such a state of body that he would have to deal [with me] drastically, which he did. But knowing what he had to work upon, he said he had no fear about my being able to stand his treatment. Between the doctor and the nurseman they pulled me through, and pleased they both were when I asked the doctor if I could go to Victoria to the hospital there. He said :

'It will take months before you are all right, and if my wife had not left to come here I would have taken the trip down with you and come back with her, but my wife has started here.' He could not leave Skagway but my Salvation Army friend got a carriage, took me down to the wharf and put me on board the C. P. R. Steamer *Tartar*, which was leaving for Victoria. He settled everything for me about passage and a berth.

The ship left that day, and on arrival at Victoria all the passangers were put on shore as the steamer left for Vancouver. After landing, the passengers all went their ways and being still unable to get about I was left with my baggage lying on the wharf for some time helpless.

At last a good Samaritan came along. Seeing me lying helpless, asked me if he could help in any way. I told him I wanted to get to St. Bridget's Hospital, if I could get a carriage. He said he would telephone from the hotel for one, which he kindly did, and in quick time a two-horse carriage came on the wharf, took me and my belongings to the above hospital. They took me in, seeing the state I was in, and put me in a first class room.

As I was not known, I had to wait till the hospital doctor came on his regular visit. In the meantime the hospital matron seeing how I was, got a nurse and between them they stripped me and put me in bed. Bringing me some hot milk, they asked if I would like anything to eat until the doctor came.

He turned out to be a friend, indeed. After examining me and after hearing my story and what the doctor at Skagway had said and done, he said;

'You are Scotch enough, and though there is far from a simple ailment on your side, I expect great help from yourself, and we will get you through. Mind, I trust you; so I expect all your help. . . .'

The hospital was a Catholic one. The nurses were all sisters from the convent, as was the matron. Learning I had been long in Japan, anytime the matron and sisters had spare time they would come in my room to hear stories about that wonderful country, Japan. My illness was inflammation of the lungs of the worst kind and being asked to talk much was against doctor's orders, but the matron and sisters would come in and get me talking about China and Japan. They never thought about the orders to keep me quiet. If it did occur to them, they would say to me, you are not going to die, you will pull through. The care they paid to me, a stranger, not being a Catholic, was above all praise. Anything I could eat, they got for me. I was some six or seven weeks in the hospital before the doctor would allow that I was strong enough to leave for the voyage back to Japan.

seventeen

RETIREMENT IN HAKODATE

IT HAPPENED that the steamer I had crossed in, was in Victoria and was to leave for Japan in two days, so I told the doctor that as I knew the captain and officers as well as the doctor on board, I would like to return with the *Pathon*. He said it was a risk, but as I had made a passage in her and knew the people, he would see the ship's doctor and tell him my trouble; so he let me go.

Being still not strong on my legs, I had to hire a carriage. Went to a barber first to get the hair off my head and face. Shorn and generally cleaned up, then went to the bank to settle about changing my money back to Japanese currency. Called at the ship's agency to engage my passage. This, with picking up my effects at the hotel where I had left them when leaving for Klondike, going back and getting my gear in the hospital, took me all the day; it was late afternoon before I got to the steamer with my gear, pretty well played out.

I was sitting on the wharf with my gear when Captain Dixon came along. Seeing me there helpless, he made the quarter master hurry up with some sailors and get me and my belongings on board. When I felt myself afloat bound to Japan, I began to pick up quickly. The ship's doctor had only to give me medicine once. On my arrival at Yokohama, before leaving for Hakodate, I consulted Dr. Munro. He went over me thoroughly and came to the conclusion that I was far from being a well man yet. He told me I would likely have some

M

setback and that I would have to take good care of myself.

Though it was well in November when I got back, I went out to Yunokawa hot springs for three weeks. Took long walks up the hills, daily getting back my strength; felt as if I was back in my native country again.

As there was no chance of getting work and I had some money matters to settle in Nagasaki, I went down there; even went as far as Shanghai. But Hakodate drew me back.

Spring coming on, I was tired of doing nothing. The Boer War was starting and I was in town looking for news about the war, when a friend of mine mentioned that the constable of the British Consulate was leaving for home and asked if I cared to apply for it.

'Get it and settle down for good,' he said. 'The pay is not much, but there is a fine house attached to the job'.

As I was getting up in years: it would settle me, he thought. It turned out so when I had applied for the place.

Though [I was] well known in Hakodate, the consul did not know [me], and being a nervous man he did not care about taking me on. He applied to the minister in Tokyo and also to the consul at Yokohama, if he could recommend a man. Luckily the consul met Mr. Wilson, the only British merchant here, and he hearing for the first [time] about the vacancy, and that I had offered for it, told the consul that he had known me for over thirty years intimately; that settled the business.

I joined the Consulate as (Temporary) Constable on St. Patrick's Day (March 17th) 1899. The 'temporary' was mentioned because sanction had to be got from the minister in Tokyo and, as it turned out later, from the Foreign Minister in London.

INDEX

Index

Index